The Good Times Are All Gone Now

The Good Times Are All Gone Now

Life, Death, and Rebirth in an Idaho Mining Town

JULIE WHITESEL WESTON

UNIVERSITY OF OKLAHOMA PRESS : NORMAN

Portions of this manuscript were published as the essay "Idaho Tailings" in *Rendezvous* (Idaho State University) 35, no. 1 (Fall 2000). Chapter 10, "We're Giving You the Special Today," was published as "Down the Mine" in *The Threepenny Review* (Spring 2005). A small portion of Chapter 8, "When the Slot Machines Went Out," was published in a short story, "Carnival," in the e-zine, *Triptych* (Autumn 2006). A portion of Chapter 16, "Look Out," was published in an essay, "The Perfect Day," in *Idaho Magazine* (November 2008).

Library of Congress Cataloging-in-Publication Data
Weston, Julie W., 1943–
The good times are all gone now : life, death, and rebirth in an Idaho mining town / Julie Whitesel Weston.
p. cm.
Includes bibliographical references.
ISBN 978-0-8061-4075-9 (pbk. : alk. paper) 1. Kellogg (Idaho)—History. 2. Kellogg (Idaho)—Social conditions. 3. Kellogg (Idaho)—Biography. 4. Miners—Idaho—Kellogg—Biography. 5. Silver mines and mining—Idaho—Kellogg—History. 6. Lead mines and mining—Idaho—Kellogg—History. 7. Bunker Hill Mining Company—History. 8. Company towns—Idaho—Case studies. 9. Kellogg Region (Idaho)—History, Local. I. Title.
F754.K45W47 2009
307.76'70979691—dc22

2009004819

The paper in this book meets the guidelines for permanence and durability of the Committee on Production Guidelines for Book Longevity of the Council on Library Resources, Inc. ∞

Copyright © 2009 Julie W. Weston. Published by the University of Oklahoma Press, Norman, Publishing Division of the University. Manufactured in the U.S.A.

For Melanie and Gerry

When you start on a long journey, trees are trees, water is water, and mountains are mountains. After you have gone some distance, trees are no longer trees, water no longer water, mountains no longer mountains. But after you have travelled a great distance, trees are once again trees, water is once again water, mountains are once again mountains.

Zen teaching

Epitaph on a tombstone, Cripple Creek, Colorado
So fleet the works of man
Back to the earth again,
All ancient and holy things
Fade like a dream.

Charles Kingsley

Contents

Illustrations

Acknowledgments

A lmost two decades ago, I decided to write about Idaho—the home of my heart. At that time, I lived in Seattle and had long ago decided I would not return to live in the town where I grew up, Kellogg, Idaho, even though I frequently visited old friends who stayed there after high school. Part of my determination arose when I attended an all-school reunion in 1986, which I describe in these pages. Another part of my determination arose when I took a writing certificate course at the University of Washington. "Write what you know" is the shopworn prescription in writing classes. Although I had practiced law for over twenty years at that point, I still felt that what I really *knew* was this town in northern Idaho.

Over the course of a decade, I interviewed many people who either lived in Kellogg or Wallace or had lived in the area, all of whom considered Idaho home. My initial intention was to write about the labor strike in the summer and fall of 1960, and I hoped to gather stories about the strike from perspectives other than mine as a teenager. Not only did I succeed in that venture, but I also learned there was much more to my town than my teenage years had taught me. I recorded and transcribed nearly all of the interviews. I wrote a novel and short stories about miners and prostitutes, eventually about sheepherders, a mossman, and other characters of Idaho. Many have been published in literary journals. Still, the interviews lived in the back of my mind. Finally, I began writing a memoir of Kellogg, weaving in the interviews, history, the strike, music, skiing, and parts of my family's life as well. My father impacted the town and the lives of my mother and us children in many ways. He, too, looms large in the story of the area.

The voices of many of my interviews find light in this book. Heartfelt thanks go to those people who lived in Kellogg and Wallace and allowed me into their lives to talk about their own histories and families. Without people like Dee and Dora Tatham, Virl McCombs, Chuck Biotti, Bob Robson, and Jim Bening, there would be no book. Many others, listed under Interviews at the back of this book, also inform my narrative. I did my best to be true to all that was told to me. I have changed a few names and combined a character or two as composites. I have drawn on my mother's memories of growing up in Idaho and her years in Kellogg to round out some of the stories and people she knew. Any errors of fact or memory, however, are my own.

Along the way, many people supported and advised me, critiqued my work, and read countless permutations of chapters, short stories, and essays or creative nonfiction pieces, for which I am grateful. My first writing group met in the fall of 1989 and continued weekly for nearly ten years. Mary Bayley, Charlene Finn, Kristen Laine, Pat Solon, and Robin Van Steenburgh read many of the chapters in this book and encouraged my efforts. More recently, on-line friends Kathie Carlson and Elaine Pinkerton Coleman and off-line friend Connie Loken read pieces or all of the manuscript and pushed me to write. My on-line writing group, Belinda Anderson, Gina Vitolo, and Anjali Bannerjee, read new versions and offered good advice.

Writing mentors—Rebecca Brown, Craig Lesley, Carolyn See, Valerie Miner, Paulette Alden, and Carol Bly—encouraged me in classes and workshops, phone and dinner conversations, and correspondence to write about Idaho and helped my craft along. An early essay about Kellogg critiqued by Gretel Ehrlich at a Yellow Bay, Montana, workshop, formed the genesis of this book. Two weeks at the Imnaha Writers' Retreat in Oregon, sponsored by Fishtrap, and a month at the Vermont Studio Center gave me time and silence and the support of fellow artists to write the first draft, which after many years and many drafts, became this final version.

I thank the University of Oklahoma Press for its endeavors to tell the stories of the American West and particularly of the history of mining. Without this Press, the literary history and times of the West would be the poorer.

Special thanks to my mother, husband and daughter, who have never ceased to believe in my writing. My daughter had her beginnings in Idaho, and although she has never lived there, she was much on my mind while writing this book. My husband read so many versions of *The Good Times Are All Gone Now* that he feels he knows everyone in it personally, although he has met only a few. His photographs and digital reproductions enhance my stories and I thank him for his help. His careful eye and sharp editing skills helped me immeasurably as have his encouragement and love.

The Good Times Are
All Gone Now

1

Toxic Town Blows Its Stack

I bought a lottery ticket. The prize? Pushing the plunger to dynamite the smokestacks rising above Kellogg, Idaho, on Memorial Day weekend in 1996. I didn't win, but my husband and I traveled from Seattle to watch the demolition of the tallest symbols of the mining industry in the town where I grew up.

Kellogg was once notorious for its brothels and gambling and famous for its lead and silver mine. Now it was noticed again for the extent and cost of its clean-up. TOXIC TOWN TO BLOW ITS STACK, reported the *Seattle Times*. The *Wall Street Journal* devoted a whole column to the event. The *Christian Science Monitor* presented a history of the town, the mines, and the extent of the environmental destruction caused by lead and arsenic emissions from the smelter and the devastation of forests and rivers during ninety-plus years of mining.

Kellogg and the people who lived there had raised me. I felt as if this event marked the destruction of some part of me that I could never recover. Who knew if the town would recover? I could point out sights and talk like a tourist guide, laughing about the smallness and apparent meanness of this little town in the Idaho Panhandle. Inside I was sad, about to bid farewell to a friend.

An hour before the scheduled destruction, we found a parking place near the outskirts of town across the valley from where the smelter once dominated the landscape. We slipped in amidst hundreds of cars, some with license plates from the local county, but most from out of state, like us. Around the corner and up a gulch, the high school I attended still opened its doors for students. We decided to climb the hillside above the former Kentucky Fried Chicken restaurant—now an alpine drive-in—to get a good view. Dozens of people carrying cameras and binoculars climbed with us on the spring morning that reminded me of all the overcast days when the smelter smoke blocked out the sun. While waiting for the show, I listened to snippets of conversation.

"What a waste!" one man said to another. Both were dressed in blue jeans and flannel shirts and both sported beards, mostly gray. If the mines had been operating, I would have identified them as miners. "We hadn't ought to let the government do this."

"That big one there is only twenty years old!" his friend said. "Stupidest thing I ever heard of." If these men were former miners, twenty years would seem brief to them. Many of my friends' fathers spent their lives working for the Bunker Hill Mining Company.

I had graduated from Kellogg High School in 1961. A number of my classmates went from school to work for the Bunker Hill Mining Company, "the Bunker" as we called it or "Uncle Bunker" as the workers often called it. Others left for college, but returned to employment in the office building, chemical labs, assay offices. Where were they now? At our first all-school reunion held in 1986, it still seemed possible to townspeople that just maybe the mine might reopen. When the tunnels flooded in the early 1990s, that hope died forever.

Those who lived in the valley could be identified by what they were saying.

"It's the last smelter in the country! We'll be defenseless in another war. Where will the lead come from for bullets?" a gray-haired woman asked her husband. He just shook his head.

"It's the end of an era," I heard.

"Now we'll just be like all other small towns—nothing unique. No symbols."

And a few bets were thrown out.

"I bet they don't fall the way they're supposed to."

"I bet they got to do the yards all over again after this." Each house in town was having its yard dug up and replaced with clean dirt. The football field had already been replaced.

"I bet in ten years they have to build 'em again."

The Environmental Protection Agency had declared the entire valley and surrounding area a Superfund Clean-up Site. The agency imposed a plan to clean up the poisons from the mining operations, and the dismantling of the buildings and destruction of the smokestacks were part of it, as well as the new dirt for yards. Without the pressure of heat and steam going up the stacks, there was the possibility they would collapse and pollute the whole townsite and beyond with the arsenic, lead, and other toxic materials laminating their insides.

"How much is this costing?" someone asked.

"Superfund Site, my ass. I've lived here all my life and I'm not full of lead poisoning."

The tallest stack, 715 feet high, had been built in the 1970s to push the sulfur dioxide emissions away from our lungs and yards and into the air currents to dissipate their effects somewhere else. Until then, the emissions were just something we all lived with. Two stacks stood 500 and 610 feet high and the smallest was only 250 feet. The tallest two were concrete and the others brick.

A carefully monitored destruction scheme was developed. The smaller stacks would be collapsed upon themselves and the bricks and mortar trucked away to be buried at a hazardous disposal site. The other two stacks would be felled, like giant trees, into ditches lined with plastic and then buried.

The last symbols of an era that began in the 1880s and ended in the 1980s were being blown up on this Memorial Day, a fitting date for the men who had worked and died in the Bunker Hill Mine and for the families who lived in Kellogg, supporting the mine for so many years. Kellogg was a town on the brink. It still teetered there, hesitating.

*   *   *

On the road into Kellogg, our first view of Silver Valley, so named by the area Chamber of Commerce to reflect the long-gone days of glory and riches, included the stacks, exclamation points for the minerals deep in the earth: *Lead! Silver! Zinc!* Mountains rose steeply on either side of Kellogg and above the remains of the industrial buildings of the mining company on the south slope. Acrid smoke no longer obscured the town. Railroad cars no longer clacked along the tracks. But other evidence of mining remained.

Red sand and clay colored the west end of the valley. Even though the sun shone between gathering clouds, an uncertain combination of water and seepage from the mine tailings, processing wastes, spread like thick gray soup across the area where we used to skate in winter. Time- and chemical-blackened stumps still dotted the surface. The tailings ponds themselves were hidden by high earth walls, like dikes, extending almost a mile along the road. When the mine smelter had been active, steam drifted from behind the embankments in summer and winter. A stream of waste poured day and night from a long pipeline leading from the smelter to the ponds. Now, nothing dropped from the lip of the pipe, and the supporting structure was broken and falling apart, like a crippled railroad trestle that would disintegrate if one more engine crossed it.

Past the slough and the dike was an empty storage yard where a lumber company once stacked timber used inside the mines to keep the earth from collapsing in, not always a successful endeavor. The largest remnant of mining marred the entrance to Kellogg—a black slag mountain of burnt dirt and sand, sharp as broken glass and almost as useless. Beside it lay Smelterville, Kellogg's "suburb," never large, but now its few houses, stores, and bars were deteriorating into shacks and vacant shells.

Above and behind the slag mountain, the complicated buildings and machinery of the smelter had mostly been dismantled. Only a few ghostly remnants remained of the once-thriving industry, including the stacks. In the old days, smoke belched; lights flashed; whistles blared. Inside this mechanical workhorse structure and the crushing plant nearby, ore was ground into powder and workers smelted down the concentrates, separating out the chaff—the tailings—and then processed the lead and silver gleanings into pigs and bars.

Directly above the smelter, horizontal lines cut bare hillsides to prevent erosion and sliding. The mountains, once devoid of trees, showed new growth from trees planted in the early 1980s after the mine closed. In fifteen years, they had grown to fifteen feet tall, still babies compared to the Douglas firs and Ponderosa pines in the mountains around Coeur d'Alene, thirty miles to the west. On the slopes of the higher peaks above Kellogg, real forests grew. Until a ski area was established, I never ventured there. Only from the gondola built to reach the ski slopes on Wardner and Kellogg peaks, its cable running almost directly over my old house, did I see the tailings ponds—squares filled with something white and goopy.

The day we came to see the stacks blown up, and for several years before, wire fences circled the slag heap and the area where the smelter, the rockhouse, the mill, the zinc and acid plants and other buildings once stood, all with large signs:

DANGER! Warning! This is a Superfund Site. No Trespassing!
KEEP OUT! Toxic materials!

During my growing-up years, my mother had parked beside the slag heap and painted mining scenes. On later visits to Kellogg, my husband and I had slipped under the fences so he could take photographs. His black-and-white photos reflected the chimneys as empty sentinels standing over abandoned buildings and twisted metal scrap heaps. Her watercolor paintings bloomed with life: smoke streaming across the valley, tanker cars lining the railroad tracks and yellow Caterpillars shoving the black slag around.

Signs along the freeway urged travelers to stop:

Visit Kellogg and Ride the Longest Gondola in the Western Hemisphere

and

Kellogg, Home of Silver Mountain and descendants of the jackass who started it all.

The comic head of a large laughing jackass adorned the latter sign, memorializing the story of how silver was discovered in the area by a prospector's burro in the 1880s.

In town, a banner stretched across a main street announcing: Kellogg, a Bavarian Village. When the mine closed, the city fathers hired a consultant who advised them to adopt a Bavarian theme. Such a move would attract a steady stream of tourists, he said, and capitalize on the ski area above town and the gondola soon to be installed. The transformation included a face-lift for all the storefronts. Indeed, several buildings had added false fronts with scalloped edges and painted alpine flowers and red ribbons, but the effort had never been adopted wholeheartedly by the business people, and the combination of empty stores, fake Tyrolean décor, and closed businesses almost made me weep. Between the black slag and the ornamental yellow roses, I wondered what visitors thought the town was doing.

Kellogg had been such a vibrant place with stores crowded by customers, trains sagging under the weight of valuable cargos rumbling through town, men going on and off shift at the mine, a daily newspaper reporting on prices of lead, silver, and zinc, and a thriving penny mining stock market. Who now remembered the hustle and bustle except those of us who grew up there? While we waited, I saw my hometown through the kaleidoscope of my growing-up years.

On dark winter mornings from 1958 to 1961, car headlights lit my trek across the valley to high school. I crunched along the snowy sidewalk past Lincoln School and down Hill Street by the football stadium. Every November 11, the whole town, wrapped in parkas, gloves, hats and boots, stuffed the stands to watch the gridiron battle between Kellogg and our archrival Wallace, a town nine miles up the valley, played out in a snowstorm where lines were invisible and numbers obliterated by mud.

I crossed the railroad tracks by the Tip Top Bar, already patronized at that early morning hour, and the houses with frosted windows—the brothels. I stopped on the bridge over Lead Creek to study the pasty water. Dogs often drowned in it. A little girl had been pulled under by the weight of the lead sludge, never to be seen again.

Along the road in Sunnyside, I passed a grocery store and a small business where a "known Communist" plied his trade, and the Sunshine Inn with the bar where my doctor father often drank and played drums when he wasn't on call at the hospital. When a representative of the Atomic Energy Commission who spoke at our high school could not get a room at the Inn because he was black, I asked my mother why. Her response was that the miners had killed two colored men several decades ago. Why had such an event occurred in my town? Only later did I understand some of the reasons, which had to do with bigotry and also with labor wars at the turn of the century when black soldiers serving in the U.S. Army had rounded up union miners and held them for months in the equivalent of a concentration camp.

Our school was new then, a modern steel and glass structure. The whole town felt pride of ownership when it appeared in Pittsburgh Glass advertisements in *Reader's Digest*. I studied Chaucer, Shakespeare, and Dickens, as well as geometry, Latin, Spanish, chemistry, and history, never thinking to link what I learned to life in the valley around me.

Before I turned up the gulch to head for classes, I stopped and looked back at snow-covered mountains, bare of trees. They had a comforting look, like giant pillows against which I could lean for support. The thousand lights of the mine buildings illuminated the sky south of my house. Pinks, neon oranges, and lavenders of the sunrise outshone the fading stars and outlined distant peaks. If the air smelled, my nose was used to it, and I didn't think of particles filling my lungs.

In those years, I thought Kellogg contained the world, and that I could stay and always be content. But I did leave, and, like others in my class, never returned to live. In the wider world, I discovered not everyone thought Communists hid under every bed, and in most places in the North at least, black people could stay in a public motel. I learned the words *dago, bohunk, wop, Okie*, and *Arkie* were pejorative, not descriptive.

On visits home after I left, I realized many of the town's limits, and my pendulum swung again: Kellogg squatted on the land like an ugly toad, and the warts of devastation wrought by mining may have rubbed off on the inhabitants. In the last decade, while researching the early days of the mining country, I found that what I thought I *knew*, both before and after leaving Kellogg, were half-truths, half-lies. There was so much more to learn.

* * *

In 1990, I began to write about the area. Part of my intention was to preserve in writing a way of life fast disappearing from the American and Northwest scenes—that of the miner and the small mining town. Part of my intention was to revisit and try to understand why Kellogg had such a pull on me, on my friends, on the people I knew growing up, and on my parents. I wanted to explore the influence several people in my life had on me, including my father, who worked at doctoring as hard as any man worked in the mines but who also drank too much, and my mother, who supported his work and tolerated his vices.

I researched the history of my own family—five generations in Idaho—and considered again my links to several special teachers. I talked for hours with my first boss, a lawyer who, with a group of courageous miners, helped end a major strike. The strike was a defining event in my life, and I wanted to know what impact it had on others in the community long after the event itself.

I interviewed people whose families came to Kellogg shortly after the turn of the twentieth century and heard them tell of their experiences and devotion to each other and to the town. I found old newspapers and magazines generated during the heydays of mining, just before and during World War I, and read about how the Bunker kept the men on during the Depression and afterwards how the mines became richer and more successful during World War II, and again in the 1950s. I interviewed friends I grew up with, their fathers and mothers, and friends of my parents—miners, businesspeople, housewives, professional people.

Until I began to write, telling stories I'd heard over the years and relating the stories from people who sometimes still lived there but more often had moved away, I had forgotten, if I ever really knew, how the mining industry supported the town. Now that the mining was gone, it was clear the town was struggling. Nor could I understand from my memories of growing up just what the men did, until I, too, went down the mine. And then my appreciation for the workers soared. Mining was not just a job, it was a calling. The miners did not desert the mines; the mines deserted them.

2

A Structural Knot

"The rocks of the Coeur d'Alene Mining District have been intensely deformed in a complex pattern . . . referred to as a structural knot."

Arthur B. Campbell and R. R. Reid, *Idaho Bureau of Mines and Geology*

Northern Idaho once was wild and green. Forests crowded the mountainsides with white pine, western cedar, fir. Blue lakes with swan, geese, ducks, rainbow and cutthroat trout, and big land-locked salmon, the Kokanee, filled glacier-gouged basins. Rivers began as rivulets high in the mountains, bringing snowmelt and rain down creeks that grew and tumbled toward the lakes, and then rushed onward to the Columbia and Snake rivers on a white-water trip to the Pacific Ocean.

Hundreds of millions of years before the beauty arrived, the mountains grew, shoved up by tectonic plate movement farther west. They shifted, sheered, and broke. Billions of tons of pressure squeezed and ground the rock, mineralizing ores in crevasses and folds deep in the earth. Then the folds bowed, fractured, and faulted in arches and strike-slip movements. Galena, sphalerite, tetrahedrite, siderite, quartz, pyrite-lead, silver, zinc, and gold-settled in veins and belts throughout an area extending twenty-five miles in the east-west direction and fifteen miles in the north-south direction in the Idaho Panhandle, along the Great Osburn Fault. This sixteen-mile right-lateral strike slip overturned to the northwest and dipped to the southwest, forming a large domelike structure—the Moon Creek–Pine Creek upwarp. Other faults converged on the

Osburn Fault, forming a gigantic structural knot with deposits along the junctions and at least one unusual attribute: the base metal ratio increases with depth. The deeper the ore shoot, the richer the vein.[1]

These mineral deposits formed what became known as the Coeur d'Alene Mining District, or the Coeur d'Alenes.[2]

Early in the 1880s, prospector A. J. Prichard arrived in the area after an arduous journey from Montana, over the mountains, through the woods, across the rivers, looking for gold. He found it. Just before the winter of 1883–84, the Northern Pacific Railroad fanned the gold rush fever in Idaho to increase its own profits by advertising gold in the streets of Prichard and Murray in eastern newspapers. For $77.18, anyone could travel from Minnesota to Montana. Thousands of men stampeded, coming the rest of the way with pack mules, horses, and wagons, struggling for days from the railhead at Missoula into deep snow and freezing temperatures to get to the back reaches of Idaho. Optimistic souls panned for gold and fought over claims and nuggets. The small settlements of Prichard, Murray, and Burke sprouted mushrooms of tents, saloons, storefronts, and mud streets.

In those days, the forests were first growth, running from horizon to horizon. Cedar stumps wider than an osprey's wingspread attest to the tree sizes. The crackle and roar of those giants crashing to the earth through dense layers of branch and pine needle surely broke the serenity of bird song and creeping animals. The tall trees became sluices for gold and lumber for houses, and later, held up the tunnels in the mines. Men's shouts and the gush of water and the tumble of rock down wooden structures reverberated in the empty spaces between trees and river.

Then the financiers and entrepreneurs moved in with more sophisticated mining techniques, changing from box sluice to dredging and hydraulics. Gold, never plentiful, ran out, but not before the riverbed had been churned and scraped and dredged and leached for every grain. The miners moved on to Burke, where the mining began to move underground.

Noah Kellogg, a prospector who was grubstaked with supplies and a burro by a storekeeper in Prichard, searched in the mountains to the west and south of Murray and Burke in 1885, looking for gold. According to legend, his mule wandered away from camp and kicked open a silver ore deposit, the beginning of what became the Bunker Hill & Sullivan mine, one of the richest mines in the country. The stampeders headed his way, populating the gulch below two mountain peaks, Milo Gulch, later named Wardner after Jim Wardner, who controlled the water rights. The settlement of Wardner spread down onto a plateau above and then along the South Fork of the Coeur d'Alene River to become the town known as Kellogg, named for old Noah.

The mining of deep gold and galena ore for silver and lead required ample pockets of capital to burrow into the earth, to build mills and then smelters for refining the metals, and to transport the wealth to markets. Small miners were squeezed out and corporations run by businessmen from San Francisco and owned by shareholders in the East developed what became a huge gold, silver, lead and zinc mining industry, reaping millions from the earth. The few exceptions, locally owned and operated, were the Hercules and Dayrock mines, begun by Henry Day, a storekeeper, and his partners. One partner was May Arkwright Hutton, an orphan, waitress, cook, and suffragette who brought the vote to women in Idaho and Washington long before the Nineteenth Amendment to the U.S. Constitution was adopted.

The miners who stayed, and a host of men who came later, labored in mines up and down the valley in Burke, Mullan, Wardner, and Kellogg and points in between as hard rock miners, dynamiting and mucking underground for $3.00 a day.

The labor wars began in the 1880s and ended in 1899 after the miners blew up the mill in Kellogg.[3] The governor of Idaho called in federal troops—black soldiers prohibited by Congress from serving east of the Mississippi—who rounded up all the miners and anyone who owned a gun, and held them in a bullpen for months. The mine owners rebuilt the mill but refused to hire any union members. Instead, they imported new men from the mines of Montana and Nevada, and also men escaping the poor and grime-filled cities and the Balkan wars in Europe. Workers came from Italy, Croatia, Serbia, Wales, Poland, Slovakia, and from the ethnic ghettoes of New York, Boston, and Chicago—a never-ending supply.

To these men, the working conditions, pay, and opportunities were far superior to those they left. If they knew of the blacklists against union members, they paid them no mind and lined up for jobs. Many were transients, living in company boarding houses for a season, and then moving from mine to mine. Others brought families from the old country and girls from the East or married saloon girls and prostitutes, built their homes, and grew their towns. Mining engineers came from all over the world, bringing ideas, culture, new inventions. They, too, settled in Kellogg and Wallace. Mine owners and engineers often lived in Wallace because there was no mine in the town, no smelter, no immediate evidence of mining itself, making for more pleasant surroundings.

Mines developed along the major belts and fault lines: Custer, Tamarack, Hercules, Anchor, Alcids, Sonora, Morning, Dayrock, Golconda, Mayflower, Alice, Lucky Friday, Vindicator, Amazon, Tiger-Poorman, Blue Grouse, Blue Bird, Big Bear, Snowstorm, to name just a few. Next to the mines, small towns grew, flourished, and then disappeared. But Kellogg remained, growing larger as the Bunker Hill Mine grew deeper and richer. Mills were necessary for processing the ore coming out of the ground because transportation costs to facilities out of state became too expensive. Before long, the economics of mining also called for a smelter, and Bunker Hill built one in 1917.

The lead smelter included three bag house sections through which stack gases and particulates from the smelting operations passed. Each section contained 400 wool bags measuring 30 feet long by 18 inches in diameter; the number of bags was later increased to 2,800 total. The bag house collected up to 90–95 percent of the particulates and these were returned to the smelting process. The rest went up the stack into the air, along with sulfur dioxide.[4] The bag house partially burned in 1974. The mine owner's decision to continue processing lead without all the bags contributed to many of the woes later suffered by the Kellogg residents.

World War I spurred the demand for lead, needed for ammunition, batteries, gasoline, pipes, and building materials. Zinc and silver, both considered by-products of lead production, grew in importance. Developing industries required both minerals: zinc for storage tanks, nails, fasteners, die-casting for locks, hinges, gauges, pumps; and silver for photography, electrical contacts and conductors, sterling ware, jewelry, dental and medical supplies.

In 1926–28, Bunker Hill built an electrolytic zinc plant to recover zinc more efficiently than its earlier processes. The purity of the new plant's product made possible a zinc die-casting business that became a large consumer of the metal. Later, a zinc fuming plant was added to recover zinc going into the slag pile, and still another plant to capture sulfur dioxide.

New finds in the 1920s and 1930s spurred mine owners to dig deeper for richer minerals, and the more they found, the deeper they dug. In 1931, a huge silver bonanza opened on the 1700 level of the Sunshine mine located between Kellogg and Wallace, at that time making it the second largest silver producer in the nation. It has since surpassed second place, becoming one of the richest silver producers in the world. Between 1884 and 1979, the Coeur d'Alene Mining District produced 907 million ounces of silver-almost five times that produced at the legendary Comstock Lode in Nevada.

The Bunker Hill mine, before it closed, had over one hundred miles of underground workings and was over a mile in depth, from 3,600 feet above sea level to 1,700 feet below sea level. As many as six thousand people worked for the Bunker at one time, and hundreds more worked in other mines up and down the valley, mining the deposits on the south side of the Osburn Fault west of the town of Osburn, where the slip occurred, and on the opposite side east of the town.

Fires swept the area in 1910, in three days burning over two million acres of eastern Washington and northern Idaho, nearly wiping out Wallace and western Montana; and again in 1931, destroying large stands of trees on the mountains around Kellogg. The mines themselves were almost as voracious for lumber, needing timbers to shore up the miles of tunnels and drifts underground. Sulfur dioxide emissions from the smelter prevented new growth. Bare dirt replaced forested slopes. In the spring, only snowberry, alder, and syringa bushes grew above Kellogg. Maple trees provided most of the greenery along the town streets during the summer months. Bunker expanded the waste ponds, building the sides up to forty feet and higher. A slag mountain grew at the edge of Smelterville, becoming a landmark along the highway. The South Fork of the Coeur d'Alene River flowed muddy gray with mine waste and tailings. It earned a new name: Lead Creek. Smelter smoke enveloped the town during temperature inversions, almost two hundred days a year, scratching the throat and burning the eyes. Grass, singed by emissions from the zinc plant and smelter, turned brown every summer.

Photos from the 1920s show a meandering river and trees growing on the hillsides. Photos from the 1960s show the bare slopes, smokestacks belching, mine buildings stair-stepping up the slopes, houses, brick buildings, cars, and activity. What the photographs don't show are the jobs and the townsfolk and their lives. Generations grew up in the town, stayed to work, left for school, returned or did not return.

On mining maps of the Idaho Panhandle, Kellogg is a small grid, like a piece of burnt toast, surrounded by the lines of dozens of rectangles and trapezoids denoting claims. The maps deceive the eye. Even haphazard geometric figures are orderly on paper. But the same lines disappear in the jumble if envisioned as laid out over mountains and canyons and gulches cut by rivers and creeks and overlaid in places by thick forests of evergreens and alder rushes. On the land, the town was still small, but giving it height, width and depth were the mine buildings and the rows of Monopoly look-alike houses and the brick YMCA and McConnell Hotel, all surrounded by woodless slopes and punctuated by the black slag mountain next to the tailings ponds.

For years, the smokestacks told the truth.

3

What Kind of Greed and Ignorance?

On a sunny July day in 1990, my mother, my husband Gerry, and I drove along the North Fork of the Coeur d'Alene River on a historical tour. We completed in a single morning the route that miners trudged for weeks a hundred years ago. Stands of pine and fir and thickets of syringa and willow crowded the mountain slopes. The mixed aromas of pitch and mock orange scented the air. My mother, born in Fruitland, Idaho, and a resident of Kellogg and Coeur d'Alene most of her life, had never visited the former gold-mining towns of Prichard and Murray. I wanted to see the old sites and remnants of the lead and silver mines in Burke and revisit the Kellogg of my youth to show my husband and to remind myself where I came from.

We almost passed Prichard without realizing it. No sign of any mining camp remained. We circled the area, certain we had missed weathered sticks of shacks or stores, a cemetery, or graveled wounds along the hillsides. The only structures we saw were two roadside taverns losing the battle against the encroaching woods. Finally, we stopped for directions and Gerry entered one of the bars. He quickly returned, coughing.

"That place was so dark, I could hardly see. Boot Hill is in Murray." He pointed up the road. "What you see here is all that's left of

Prichard. My god, those people were smoking Camels and knocking back beers at ten in the morning!"

Along the road to Murray, behind a screen of young evergreens, hundreds of house-sized gravel mounds lined the river. This was no natural phenomenon. These were the remnants of the hydraulic and dredge gold mining operations last quitted around 1917. They led us to the living remains of the town—two bars with their doors open and country music, a lament to lost love, jangling in the morning sun; a museum of dusty mining tools and liquor jugs stenciled with the message "Return to A&W Whiskey for Refill"; a single gas pump, where tourist cars from Indiana and Texas waited to fill up; and a dozen ramshackle houses.

We inched past the storefronts and stopped to take photographs. A tin replica of a railroad lamp hung above one doorway, the original "red light" for brothels in the Panhandle. Past a vacant lot stood the old county courthouse. Two narrow stories high, it had aged in fading clapboard dignity, reminding both Gerry and me of the people who practiced law before we did, perhaps setting legal precedents we used in our own work.

Here in the days of gold, hearings and trials settled claim disputes, quieted titles, established boundary lines, and allocated shares. A store owner who grubstaked a prospector with food, picks, shovels, gold pans, and pack animals was entitled to 10 percent of a find. Unless outcroppings and claims were posted in the proper manner, anyone could jump the workings and be legal. Who sought gold where on the river and how much dredging and sluicing each claim was entitled to, occupied the legal minds in the courthouse. It stretched my imagination to think of the courtroom—there could be only one in the pinched building with one doorway—filled with a judge, lawyers, parties of the first and second parts, witnesses, a clerk or bailiff, and onlookers. People must have been shorter, narrower, smaller than they are now. The pound of the gavel would have been heard next door at the saloon, perhaps even across the street at the assay office. Or not at all, being drowned out by the mining operations. The gravel mounds stood as mute testimony of the miners' labors. A few dilapidated structures perched on a cliff cut by high-powered water streams. I wondered if anyone stood up in the courthouse to object, as someone would today, when the gobbling machines ate right down Gold Street, spitting out rocks and houses and flowers and lives.

The ghosts of Murray hunkered in a shady glen across the river in the cemetery. Gray, weathered boards and ancient tombstones marked the graves of whom? Whatever words were carved or etched for the ages had eroded or melted away in a century of winter storms.

A few granite stones still told stories: of men who died young, of children who were struck down in the influenza epidemic of 1918, of mothers who passed in their early thirties, and of pioneers who stuck it out until the 1950s and '60s. Some boards had been re-newed and re-inscribed. One was Sacred to the Memory of Maggie Hall, Molly-B-Dam, Died at Murray, Jan. 17, 1888, Age 35 Years, always known in story lore as the Prostitute with the Heart of Gold. One was for Terrible Edith, another prostitute whose name still crowns a mining claim in the mountains beyond the graveyard.

We read in whispers Molly B'Dam's inscription or called quietly to each other to come see. Beside us thrummed the river, a solemn song. A kingfisher flitting from tree to tree and a patch of blue sky lightened our mood as we climbed back into our car.

"It's hard to believe five thousand people lived here. Where are they all buried?" my husband asked.

"The miners deserted Prichard and Murray," I answered. "They headed for Burke, and it's in such a narrow canyon, the railroad tracks filled the main street. Shopkeepers had to pull in their awnings when the ore train passed. The Tiger Hotel straddled the tracks, and the train ran through it. I've seen old photos of Burke. Wallace and Kellogg, too. Houses and tents covered the hillsides."

"When I came to be with your father in early 1947, hardly anyone lived up these gulches anymore," my mother said. "I took an excursion trip to Burke sometime in the '50s with our ladies' study club. The old Tiger Hotel was boarded up but still standing, and of course, all the mines were in operation then. They crowded out the houses, I guess. Those were boom days, and they lasted through the 1970s."

"You'd think the silver would have run out," Gerry said. He and Mother talked to each other in the front seat. I sat behind and avoided looking over the drop-off of the mountain pass we were traveling through.

"The lead and silver mines were some of the richest in the world," my mother said. "Lead and zinc were used in car batteries and paint. With everyone buying houses and cars after the war, there was more money to dig deeper."

"Don't forget bullets," I added.

Mother continued as if I'd said nothing. "And then the Korean War and the Cold War. The mines and smelter meant we could fight anywhere in the world and not depend on anyone else. Everyone in town bought penny stocks, hoping to get rich. Julie's father sold his Lucky Friday stock for a piano for the children." The Lucky Friday is one of the few mines that still operates in the Coeur d'Alenes.

"He should have sold the Nabob stock instead," I piped from the back seat.

"Old-timers say there's still silver down there. It just costs too much to bring it out," Mother said.

In the Idaho Panhandle, mining and logging supported for decades the small towns and the state treasury. Little is left of either industry. The owners and workers took too much, too soon, always thinking there were more trees and more mountains and more veins of ore to exploit. Almost no one realized or considered that an end might come—to the natural resources, to the tariffs that protected the products from cheaper imports from South America, to the lack of concern about the environment, and to the unregulated private ownership.

During our drive, we passed mile after mile of closed and crumbling mine operations—Yellow Dog, Star-Phoenix, Tamarack, Gem-Hecla, Tiger-Poorman—the only remaining tangible evidence of the lines on the claim maps. A sign at the entrance to Burke, dusty and derelict in the sun, described the old Tiger Hotel as the only structure in the country to have two railroads, a road, and a stream run through its center.

Deserted mills with trashed vehicles disintegrating in their yards, shattered glass, and collapsed and rusty structures—now no more than stacks of tired lumber and steel beams blackened by soot, sun, and rain—presided over tailings spills down the canyon walls into Canyon Creek. A palette of colors from the remnants of chemicals and waste rocks, brown and copper and iridescent orange and green and purple, splotched the hillsides. In Kellogg, scummed tailings ponds, a mountain of black slag, lead-poisoned earth, and tainted water remain. These are the mining legacy.

My husband, a native of Washington and an ardent flyfisher, could hardly believe the devastation. "What kind of greed and ignorance does this? How could you live here?"

"It wasn't greed," my mother answered. "Besides, if it weren't for Bunker Hill, there wouldn't have been a kindergarten. Or all those jobs. People talk about how poor things were, but Julie's father went into those houses. They had TVs just like everybody else." My father did make house calls and sometimes I went with him and waited in the car.

"Those children who had lead poisoning," Mother continued, "must have eaten the dirt."

Yet, blaming greed or even ignorance is too simple. I knew the people and institutions. Conversations in the cafes had centered on our economy, the likelihood of and hope for new and richer veins of ore, metals prices, the speed and skill of the Damiano boys on the basketball team, and the school bond issues, which always passed. No one went hungry in my town, although there undoubtedly was more poverty than was apparent. My father never turned away a patient.

The working men supported their families and dozens of businesses with the money they earned. My mother, like the remaining residents of the area, remembers the largesse of Bunker Hill: modern gymnasiums and chemistry labs, uniforms and instruments for the band, summer jobs for students, a free ski program for children, and hundreds of scholarships to college. These are also part of the mining legacy.

An assay scale weighs precious metals to determine worth. How do we weigh the value of metals as compared to the value of lives and how they're lived? Or the value of clean water and forested lands as compared to the value of jobs? These are not easy tasks.

4
Work and Good Pay

The cemetery on the hill above Kellogg has a separate section crammed with headstones for Italians from Besano. That small town, within shouting distance of the Swiss border, was the source of one of the largest groups of immigrants to work in the Bunker Hill mine. Rinaldis, Bottinellis, Vergobbis, Biottis, Gasperis—names on the headstones—were all families who arrived in northern Idaho at the turn of the twentieth century and still populate Kellogg.

When Joe Rinaldi was nine, he went to work in Milan, Italy, as an apprentice stone mason, carrying mortar up ladders for the cathedral. As a journeyman stone mason, he traveled to Belgium, Germany, and France, seeking work and returning to Italy in the winter. There, he and other stone workers made their own wine and sat in cantinas, drinking. He had a wife to support and two children, Jessie and Charles.

His wife's uncles had emigrated to northern Idaho before 1900. They wrote to Joe: "Come to Kellogg. There's work and good pay and a good place to live." In 1909, he followed them and, a year later, sent money home to bring his wife and children to him.

Travel by steerage across the ocean was all the Rinaldis could afford. On the ship, little Jessie, only four years old, ran away from her mother to explore. She crawled up a railing to watch the water foam and swirl. Her foot slipped. Her mother grabbed her arm and pulled her away from the ship's dumping station. At Ellis Island, Jessie wandered off again. All the people wearing dark brown coats, black dresses, an occasional brightly colored scarf, and carrying bags and bundles sparked her curiosity. Where did they come from? A tall man in a uniform with gold buttons reached out to her and she turned and ran, right into the elbow of a woman trying to keep her children gathered about her. By the time Jessie found her own mother again, her face was swollen and a black eye bloomed.

When the doctor examined Jessie, he suspected she had an eye disease and marked the back of her coat with a chalked X. Friends in Italy had warned Mrs. Rinaldi: "They're very particular. If there's anything wrong at all with you, you don't get in." A practical woman, Mrs. Rinaldi took her handkerchief and rubbed the X off the back of Jessie's coat. Then she and her two children followed everyone else off the island.

The train trip west was another long voyage with little money. Mrs. Rinaldi bought apples from the conductor and split them between the two children. She had never seen anyone with black skin, and she said to Jessie, "My goodness, his collar isn't dirty. You'd think that would rub off on his beautiful white shirt." Sometimes, they bought sandwiches at railroad restaurants. When Mrs. Rinaldi saw skeletons of cows beside the tracks, she worried: "What kind of a country are we getting into?" The high trestles scared her.

After days on the train, they finally arrived in Wallace, the main depot for the Northern Pacific Railway, and were met by Joe. They took the spur line to Kellogg, nine miles west down the valley, and moved into a small house rented from one of the uncles. Mrs. Rinaldi was shocked because it was only one story. In Besano, Italy, she was used to tall houses with fifteen-foot ceilings. "Well, I'll starve if I have to stay here," she said. "I'll smother."

Neither Jessie nor Charles, who was two years older, could speak any English when they arrived. "My mother's cousins made fun of my mother," Jessie said. "They wondered why she sent my brother to school when he couldn't even speak the language, and she said, 'What better place is there to learn than at school?' "

* * *

"My father was a stonemason," Charles explained. "He built some of the walls in Glacier National Park. The Bunker released him for a couple of months in the summertime. When the first Italians came to America, they all settled in New York because they worked on the Hudson River, lining it with rock and cement. Then they found out about the mine here, how easy it was to live. The Italians came. The Swedes came. Yugoslavians. They got good pay compared to what Italy paid, and what they made on the Hudson River."

Stone masonry was not what the Bunker Hill Mine in Kellogg or the Hercules and Morning mines in Burke and Mullan needed. Joe Rinaldi hired on to unload rail cars of brick in the Bunker Hill yard. His next job was on the crusher in the rock house, where the ore brought out in cars was dumped onto a grid of rails. The men swung big sledgehammers to break the ore through the grizzlies and into the crusher.

"When the carload was empty," Jessie said, "his little boss—he was just about as little as my dad was—would send him home. No matter what time of day it was, maybe it was before noon. My dad always took his lunch in case he could stay and work. But that boss would say, 'OK Joe, there isn't anything more for you to do.' My dad went home and he told my mother's aunt, 'I'm going to play dumb. I'm not going to understand him the next time he tells me to go home. I'm going to find something to do and I'm going to start working.'

"So the next time, his boss told him he could go home, my dad grabbed the broom on the warehouse porch and started sweeping. The boss went over to another one of the shift bosses and said, 'What am I going to do with that damn wop? I told him to go home and he won't go.' The other one said, 'If I had a man that wanted to work that badly, I'd never send him home.' So his boss never sent my dad home again."

After his family arrived, Joe came home with money from working for Bunker Hill and put it on the table.

"Joe, where did you get all that money? You didn't steal it, did you?" His wife had never seen so much at one time. Except for what she needed to run the house, she traded the money at the bank for gold. Eventually she had a big Calumet baking powder can full of gold coins, hidden under the cellar steps. With this money, they built a house in 1918.

Decades later, Charles Rinaldi and his wife, Rose, lived in a wood frame structure that replaced his father's house on the same lot along Division Street in Sunnyside, the part of town north of the river. On shelves and tables in their neat living area, the faces of children, grandchildren and great-grandchildren looked out from frames and folders. Most had dark curly hair, brown eyes, olive skin, although Charles was pale-skinned and now almost bald. He wore glasses and had the serious look of a man who worked with numbers. Rose made small, quick movements with her hands when she served coffee. She sat on the edge of the davenport. With his legs stretched out in front of him and crossed, Charles sat in an easy chair by the window looking out on the street. He had retired from his job as an accountant for the Bunker in 1969, twenty-two years earlier. He looked much younger than his age: eighty-six years.

His sister, Jessie, was the mother of two of my friends and classmates. Her family lived half a block from our house in Kellogg. She was tinier and rounder than I remembered her, but her dark eyes still sparkled with humor and she grinned like a twelve-year-old tomboy.

Charles spent his first paycheck on his sister's teeth. Charles began working at the Bunker while in high school. After graduation, he worked at the rockhouse, following in his father's footsteps. "That was in 1923," he said. "My job was breaking rock and picking out wood. Small pieces could go through, but the wedges—you know what they are—they're about that thick," he said, holding his thumb and forefinger apart, "and they'd use them in the mines to wedge up timber. Sometimes they'd get in with the ore and stop the crusher. Then the rock traveled on conveyor belts across the road into the mill. I made $3.75 a day."

I imagined broken arms and crushed fingers in the "crusher," although of course it was named for the crushing of rock. The process hardly changed over ninety years, but now the buildings were burned or gone. There were two roads into town—one in the lower valley along the river leading into Sunnyside and the other on the plateau that passed the mine entrance and became McKinley Avenue as it entered town. The upper road was lined on either side by industrial buildings: the mill, the rockhouse, the motor pool, the maintenance offices. In between the mill on one end and the smelter on the other, were ramshackle houses taken over by Okies and Arkies when they moved to town to get jobs. They formed another wave of immigrants in the 1930s and '40s, similar to the European immigration a generation earlier.

"When we came in 1910, I bet there wasn't fifteen houses in Sunnyside," Charles said. "There was the depot, because the narrow-gauge railroad used to run up on Mission Avenue. And the old Bottinelli house was a saloon. We built a little house here." He pointed to the floor. "There was a school house where the King Electric is now. The Vergobbi house is there." He pointed next door. "There was the Patterson house, then the Bottinellis. Mostly Italians. Of course the trees were really full in that time."

Their house was across the street from the old Rena Theatre, closed and boarded up. I thought about the rows of red plush seats and seeing *Murders in the Rue Morgue, The Bodysnatchers, To Hell and*

Back, and *Quo Vadis.* The Rinaldis' children and nieces and nephews were part of the crowd that stood in lines outside the Rena every Friday night.

"The river used to run down Riverside Avenue instead of where it is now," Charles said. "I can't recall how it was moved, but two years in a row, it broke out and came right down Riverside again where the schoolhouse was. It went through a little forest. The flume from Big Creek—that's where Bunker got its water—was over there by the Copper Keg. Piped it all the way down."

For most of the town's existence, the round rusty-looking pipe about a foot in diameter carried water along the hillside on an elevated wood-piling system above the river, extending the three miles from Big Creek east of town to the Bunker. Water for the town itself came partly from the Big Creek area and partly from Milo Creek, running through Wardner, and always tasted clean and fresh. After one woman told me how the mortuary used to embalm bodies in a little tent next to Milo Creek, I wondered just how clean the water really was.

Charles Rinaldi married Rose during the Depression and toward the end of Prohibition. "There were no saloons but everybody made their own liquor," he said. "My dad made wine every year. In those days you used to get grapes and crush them. It was against the law, but he did it anyway.

"We'd smash the grapes with our hands, getting red up to here." Charles pointed to his elbow and laughed. "Then we'd put them in a big wooden barrel. When it starts to ferment, the grapes rise and the juice stays on the bottom. We'd leave it like that for eight or nine days, then take a plunger and push the grapes down into the juice. Then, oh about the last week, we let the grapes come up. They'd dry out because all the juice had gone down. We'd take the wine out and put it in casks. My dad used to take a spoon at the bunghole of the barrel, taste the wine, clean it off, and in the spring of the year, he'd seal it up.

"Fifty-gallon barrel. Big. We used oak barrels, got them from Canada, old whiskey barrels. We made wine with Concord grapes. If some of them were spoiled, we'd just smash them anyhow and put them in. When they were fermented all the poison would come out of them. My dad used to drink a glass of wine every night for supper. Good old 'Dago Red.' I don't drink it in the summer time. I drink it in the winter, when it gets cold."

Dago Red bottles of wine entered my own house via patients who gave them to my father, along with elk steaks, venison, and salmon from the coast, welcome gifts because Dad didn't hunt or fish. I remembered trying to drink some, but it was sour, not like the sweet wine at Episcopal Communion. I mentioned this to the Rinaldis, but I didn't tell them how often he drank it.

Kellogg was full of big Italian families. Every summer they organized a picnic up Moon Gulch, with wine, several kegs of beer, roast beef and chicken, platters of food and desserts. During the Depression, the mining shifts were cut down to three days a week. "We didn't have any problems," Rose said.

* * *

Chuck Biotti, the father of my friend Diane, was born in this country, but his father had emigrated from Italy to work in the mines and then sent for his wife, the same pattern followed by the Rinaldis and other immigrants. He described growing up in Kellogg in nostalgic terms.

"We used to go fishing up Big Creek," he said, pronouncing the word "creek" as "crick," something we all did. "When the fish weren't biting we'd pick up golf balls in the creek. Wade out there and go over to the country club and sell them, half a shopping bag full. We sold them for ten cents apiece. The golf course was up there for years where the settling pond is now."

The only golf course I remembered was west of town near Pinehurst. The idea of people playing golf up Big Creek in the 1920s surprised me, but Chuck assured me the course existed a long time until the settling pond replaced it and a new one was rebuilt on a nearby plateau. Golf and mining were incongruous to me. In the mid-1950s my mother insisted I take lessons at the Pinehurst golf course, where we often went for potluck dinners on Friday nights. While we kids played Red Rover, throwing a ball over the roof to the other side, it never occurred to me then that miners might be working several thousand feet under the grass—sweating and drilling, setting off dynamite, loading ore into cars.

"A bunch of us used to chum around together. If we had twenty-five or thirty cents in our pockets, we'd go to the depot and catch the passenger train in the morning, ride it up to Wallace for a quarter round trip and bring it back in the afternoon." Chuck told this story while sitting in his daughter's living room. He gestured directions with his arm and pulled coins out of his pocket to show me. "Or we'd take the freight train to Prichard where it picked up ore cars at the Jack Waite Mine. For seventy-five cents, we could ride on up to Coal Creek and sometimes walk home, about nine miles. We always brought fresh vegetables to the prospector who lived there, and he had a whole bunch of mattresses laid out on the floor. We'd sleep until four in the morning, get up and pick five or six gallons of huckleberries. Other times we'd walk up cemetery road and then up to the Alhambra Mine, about four or five miles, pick huckleberries and bring them home to sell for 75 cents a gallon."

Chuck was well into his eighties when we talked, still picking huckleberries for friends and family and still gathering greens for the local flower shop. I mentioned wine-making.

"There's not many making that Dago Red anymore. During the Prohibition days everybody, not only Italian, over there on Sunnyside was making it. Do you remember Radovich? The guy that shot his wife in bed and shot himself? The two boys, they would make twenty-five, thirty-gallon barrels of different kinds of wines in the basement. It was first-class wine, every one. Some was grape.

Some was cherry. Those kids said, 'Dad wants you to come over to the house before we leave.' So we went over. 'Try some of this,' he'd say. By the time you got halfway through the sampling process, you were darn near two sheets under the wind. But boy, he made real good wine.

"It was against the law to make it. They had a lot of federal agents in plain clothes, and if you got caught, you served time in jail. Peter R—— got caught with about one hundred gallons—two big barrels. The federal agents raided your place with a search warrant. If they found a fifty-gallon barrel, whether it was in your front room, your kitchen or down in the basement, they had a hammer in their hand and knocked out the goddam cork and fifty gallons of wine would spill all over the place. They'd destroy it right there and haul you off to Coeur d'Alene. Peter served thirty days in jail plus a five hundred dollar fine. Only wine I ever made was rhubarb, right here, two gallons."

* * *

Chuck Biotti's and the Rinaldis' stories reflect the experiences of men who came to Kellogg, drawn by the mining jobs, from Finland, Wales, Poland, Croatia, England, Hungary after the uprising in 1956; from Mexico, and from both eastern and western states in America. The early miners, particularly gold miners, rushed to the rumored source of wealth as they did in Prichard and Murray and then left. Men like Joe Rinaldi and Chuck Biotti's father came, stayed, brought their families. Father to son, the tradition of the mines continued. Charles Rinaldi worked forty-six years for Bunker Hill, and his father worked as long. Charles couldn't speak English when he began and became an accountant. His story was typical. Although many miners were transients, moving from workings in Butte, Montana, to Idaho and on to Nevada, enough craved the security of permanent jobs and homes to make Kellogg and Wallace thriving communities for almost one hundred years.

5

A One-Horse Town

Not all the early immigrants into northern Idaho arrived from Europe. Transient miners moved from mining camp to mining camp throughout the West. Many came from Butte, Montana, during its labor strife, or left Nevada to follow rumors of rich silver strikes in the Coeur d'Alenes. The industry drew others who depended indirectly upon the mines for their livelihoods. They logged, opened cafes, ran butcher shops and grocery stores, provided rooming houses and boarding houses, or operated small businesses to serve the miners and their families.

* * *

Jim Bening's father moved from Troy, Montana, to the Kellogg area early in the twentieth century. He had been a logger in Wisconsin, and when all the timber was cut, he moved west to Montana and then on to Alaska, where he trapped marten, mink, and beaver. After two years he returned to Montana, in time to work as a forest ranger during the 1910 fire. Jim's mother told him that his father came home from the fire with "his tongue all swoll up because he hadn't drank for such a long, long time."

In Idaho, Jim's father went into logging again, a business Jim took up in the 1950s after working in the mines during the late '30s and '40s. Their first house with a bathroom, or as Jim phrased it, "a shitter and a bathtub indoors," was in Kellogg, when Jim was twelve. By the time he was fifteen, Jim drove a Studebaker bus with side curtains, carrying miners, drunk from weekend sprees, to the Tamarack Mine above Wallace and stopping at the boarding houses for free food. He got the job driving the miners because he played football and the head of Hecla Mining liked to help athletes. Jim went to college and returned to the mines in the Depression, the only place he could get a job.

Jim's background was mostly English. "Italian people and a lot of Welsh lived in Kellogg. They were fabulous people. During the Depression, they kind of looked after one another. Up in Burke it was Irish, and Mullan was Finlanders. They were wonderful ax men. They'd go up to Fin Gulch and build a log house. After that, first thing you know they sent for their families and here comes a wife and two or three kids."

One of my father's best friends, Jim spoke to me by telephone when he was dying of cancer. For years, I'd heard his stories and I wanted him to tell them one more time. His voice was gravelly, as always, and by phone, I could think of him as he had been, ruggedly handsome with black hair going gray, muscled arms as if he had been out in the forests sawing down trees his whole life, a little round in the middle as he aged, and with a smile almost as wide as his face. One of the first things he said when we talked was that he was worried about my mother. "I don't want to ever pry, but what worries me—I just don't want her to run out of money." If I'd said she was having a hard time, which she wasn't, he would have mailed a check to her that very day. Generous and gruff, he was typical of so many of the men I knew in Kellogg.

"Julie, you're going to have a fabulous time sorting it out. It's been a fabulous company, the Bunker. It was a one-horse town," he said, speaking of Kellogg, "all the different people that associate together. You could always get a job there. Everybody mixed and had a pretty good time without any class consciousness. I always appreciated the fact that there was no clannishness in Kellogg.

"There's quite a few things I could tell you that I know for sure, but I can't tell you over the telephone. If you put it in a book, someone might kill you yet." Sadly, Jim died before I could visit him. The rest of his stories were left to my imagination.

* * *

Eulah Chilcott's father came to Kellogg from Oregon. He drove ore trucks from the mine entrance in Wardner down Corduroy Hill, so named because of the logs placed in it to cut down on the mud, to the mill. He married her mother in 1903 and built a home in Wardner.

In 1923, Eulah worked at the Pleasant Home boarding house serving meals to miners. "We girls had rooms downstairs. The rooms were rather rugged, but it was nice. We didn't have much place to hang clothes, only on the wall.

"My husband Earl's mother cooked up here when I first met him. His brother had been killed in the mine in his senior year. Earl was in California working and his mother didn't want him to come back. One day I went down the street and he was washing windows at the Pleasant Home and yodeling and singing." Earl also played saxophone in Kelly's City Band.

"We got married in Moscow in 1929. I had a nice dress from Christmas so I wore that. It was black with fuchsia flecks and had a beautiful lace collar and ecru cuffs. We took a honeymoon trip to Lewiston, for a week, and then we came back. Earl was working in the Inland Cigar Store, bartending." This was during Prohibition.

"The band practiced at City Hall and played around town. They had dancing recitals and concerts and style shows. At the union hall there was a dance every Saturday night and also at the Odd Fellows Hall downstairs."

Eulah worked at the Davenport Cafe before her son Troy was born. Although she had been to business school in Spokane, she didn't use the typing and shorthand skills she'd learned. "During the Depression we were buying a little house. We paid five dollars every once in a while and we finally got it paid off. Everybody really had a hard time. We made about two dollars and fifty cents a day. Earl would be off for a day and we decided that I would go back to the cafe and he would take care of Troy. They weren't paying that much then, about eleven cents an hour. So Earl said, 'You better quit.' "

In spite of the hardships, the Chilcotts bought one or two shares of stock in the Coeur d'Alene Mines every week for twelve cents a share. Earl eventually bought the Inland Cigar Store when the owner wanted out, and he became a large shareholder in the Coeur d'Alene Mines, one of the more successful mining companies.

"The Inland Cigar Store. In those days, they really gambled. They had the slot machines, poker, all kinds of gambling games. During one Miners Picnic, I always remember, the owner had emptied his slot machines. He had an old suitcase, one of those satchel types, lifted it and the handle broke off. You may not believe this, but Earl was in that business from the time we married until he was sixty-five and I was never in there or drew a glass of beer. Earl didn't believe in women being in there. It was a real old-fashioned place. It had big high ceilings and great big globe lights like in schoolhouses. In the back room he had gambling tables with green velvet tops. They had a big pool table and card tables covered with green. There was a little fountain out front with four stools. They were known for making the best milkshakes in town."

Eulah played bridge with my mother in the Kellogg Bridge Club, whose members became such only by invitation. She lived in a large house about a block off Main Street, one with dark wood exterior and gables and dark beams inside, designed by a Spokane architect named Cutter. We sat in a quiet corner of a living room filled with what I thought of as antique furniture—heavy, well-upholstered, rich-feeling.

In the 1980s, to take a trip to Arizona before Earl died, Eulah said they sold some stock at eighteen dollars a share. She and her husband outlived their son and daughter, who both died of cancer as adults. And then Earl died in his late sixties.

* * *

Dolly Parker and her husband, Gordie, bought an orchard near Coeur d'Alene. When it frosted every year, Gordie traveled to Kellogg to get a job and a room. Dolly joined him in 1913. "Of all the terrible places that God ever created, it was this town. Mud all over the streets. They'd bring the horses down from Wardner with the ore and they put planks on the sidewalks so you could cross from one side to another. Boy, a regular pig run. But Gordie got work."

Her name fit her. Dolly's features were as delicate as a porcelain china doll's, even in her eighties, but her deep, robust voice belied the fragility of her figure.

For a while, they lived up Deadwood Gulch. "It was up the mountain, way above the smelter. We used to pay ten cents to drive down to Kellogg on the bobsled. It left every hour-and-a-half. Great big bobsled. You could see sparks off the rocks when you went down."

Dolly was mostly blind when I met with her. She rocked as she talked. Her house was still except for a clock ticking. An aroma like faded roses wafted from the plastic flowers in the middle of her dining table. "Did you know they had orange trees in the hoist room? Old Mr. Tregoning spit some orange seeds out and a couple months later here come a little orange tree growing up in the mine. There's a lot of history in this country. Some of it's funny and some not so funny." She fingered the apron gathered in her lap and laughed, a low throaty chuckle.

"We had lots of fun. We had dances every Saturday night at the

Old Wardner Hall. Boy oh boy. Gordie played the fiddle and someone sat at the piano and we all wore housedresses. The old building
would just shake.

"When the men in the mine got in an argument, they'd come
out at night and fight at the ball ground so everybody would come
and watch. Got some pretty good fights that way." She rocked and
thought. "There isn't no better place to live than right here. Don't
have tornadoes. Don't have, well, we did have one bad flood, one
year at Christmas time. It took all the bridges out from here to
Wallace but one, and that was the condemned one. Now that's the
truth."

6

The Sky Was the Limit

In the years following the end of World War II, more people came to Idaho for the jobs. Few of these new residents were immigrants from Europe. Most had lived elsewhere in the United States, often working in mines.

Dora and Ira D. (Dee) Tatham arrived in Kellogg in 1950. Dee had worked all over the West—in gold, silver, lead, and uranium hardrock mines in Colorado, phosphate in Utah, and also as a carpenter for the Hanford site in Richland, Washington. Occasionally, he labored farther afield—in Adak, Alaska, and Thule, Greenland. But he spent the most years mining lead, zinc, and silver in the Bunker Hill Mine, drilling underground and setting dynamite, becoming an expert powderman or "powder monkey." Dora worked as a cook and then manager of Pat's Boarding House and, for a few years, of her own boarding house—the Pleasant Home. Eventually, she bought Pat's and operated it with Dee's help when he wasn't underground and after he retired. They raised a family of six children— five daughters and one son. Their third daughter, Betty, and I grew into fast friends after we met each other in the eighth grade.

"When we first came here, we couldn't get a place to live at all," Dora said. "We camped down there at Shoshone Park, out under the stars. Dee couldn't go to work until we got an address. After about a week and a half, we got into a little cabin, at the other end of Wallace. It had a bedroom and a two-by-four kitchen. We had the five kids with us. Our oldest was in California. Boy were we lucky—it just rained down that night, and we'd been sleeping out before that. Then Dee went to work and we got a house in Smelterville. We had to stay in that cabin a month before we could get in a house. Old Ted Brown, he was the realtor then. We went to him and he says, 'Are you working at Bunker Hill?'

"'Yeah, just started today.' If you worked at Bunker Hill, they financed the house for you. It was the first time we ever got a house, and Dee had just worked one shift. When we first came to Kellogg, the sky was the limit. You could go and charge anything you wanted as long as you said you worked at the Bunker.

"And there were slot machines in the restaurants, in the bowling alley, in the bars and cafes and everywhere. Gambling every night, every night they had a dollar.

"So then Dee worked at Bunker—that was in 1950—and the spring of '51. In 1951, he went to Adak, Alaska. Old Charlie Simmons came hot-footing it down there after Dee quit. 'What are you going to go there for?' he asked. And Dee says, 'I can make more money.' I told him Dee intended to come back. 'Well, we just want to know,' Charlie Simmons said. [Later] when Dee went to Greenland, they never said anything."

I remembered Betty's father being gone a lot. Thin and dark-complected, he rarely spoke to us, except to kid around, and was often dressed in an undershirt and long pants around the house on weekends, just like my grandfather. Her mother, a strong, compact woman, usually wearing a white uniform, thick-soled white shoes, and a cardigan sweater, seemed always to be working. Betty helped with the younger kids at home and often cooked family meals.

"When Dee went to Adak, he went up in May and come back in November. When he went to Greenland, he went six or eight months. The workers couldn't stay the year around in Greenland on account of the weather. That was in 1953. He went twice. Was there a strike in '56? He went up that time, too. He went three or four times, because of the pay. It cut his pension, too, when he quit Bunker Hill. The last time he went to work was fifteen years ago. He'd had about twenty-five years in Bunker if he hadn't been going all those places."

Dora worked at Pat's Boarding House for twenty-four years, beginning in 1951. She bought it after the 1960 strike and finally sold it in 1975.

"Not all the men lived at the boarding house. They stayed in Quonset huts down by the dairy. The ones who lived at Pat's, the biggest majority of them were single. I didn't know nothing like these men. How wild they were, drinking. This guy came in for breakfast one morning. He wore his lumberjack pants, the big black pants with suspenders, and he was in his undershirt and his pants fell down. I never knew anything like that ever happened. I got educated.

"They'd drink in their rooms any time they could. They'd go downtown and spend all their money and go to their rooms, drinking. Did you ever hear of Cooley D——? He was a periodic drunkard. He'd go for two or three years without drinking and then when he got on one, boy."

"That was the guy we called 'Three Toes' down in the mine," Dee added. "He chopped two of his toes off with an axe."

"He stayed up there in his room and drank too much," Dora said. "Anyhow they had to get an ambulance and took him to the hospital. One morning I went to work and there he was, outside the boarding house. They'd taken his clothes in the hospital and wouldn't let him have them. So there he was standing in his hospital gown and bedroom slippers, wanting to go in when I got there at 4:00 in the morning. And then he got drunk again.

"And the year of the strike there was one guy, they called him Sanitary Pete. He used to be in the Army and you could bounce a quarter on his bed. He found out he had cancer of the bone, and he went down to one fellow that had a .38 German Luger, and he went into his room. He got a big load on and come up and was splattered all over the little washroom up there. Shot himself."

"Whiskey Joe was the one who came down and said Pete shot hisself," Dee said. "If I ever catch up with Pete, I'm going to tell him by god next time he blows his head off, don't do it in the utility room."

* * *

In one way or another, nearly everyone was drawn to Kellogg because of the mining. First jobs were usually in the mines or related to mining. Bunker Hill and other operations up the valley provided the work, the houses, the means for entertainment and for supporting families. My interviews were with people from all walks of life and every one talked of how they loved Kellogg or Wallace. Nearly all had come from humble origins. They worked hard to earn money, struggled, and overcame many hardships. Some bought mining stock or opened their own businesses, often both. All of them remembered good times. When they talked about the bad times, they laughed and shook their heads at having come through all right. All commented on the remarkable people who lived in the towns of the Panhandle, how they worked together, played together, competed with each other, cared for each other.

Few said anything about the surroundings—how the trees had disappeared from the slopes of the mountains, how only maple trees grew in town and only shrubbery on the hills, how smelter smoke clogged the air, how gray was Lead Creek, how tall grew the mountain of slag. Most reported on how rich the mines were, how much money was taken from the mountains, how the mines provided jobs for anyone and everyone, how many scholarships were awarded each year.

Jim Bening perhaps conveyed the feeling best: "You liked to feel you were part of the community, do your part whatever it was. I think a lot of people felt that way. A lot of very gracious people came out of there, willing to share a little bit with everybody."

Clearly, Kellogg was an endeavor, as well as a place, in which everyone participated.

7

"Yo ho ho, You and Me"

As my mother's mother, Grandmother Elsie, lay dying, she told me of one late-summer adventure at Josephus Lakes in central Idaho. Amidst the anesthetic smell of her hospital room, her age-speckled arms described the motion of horses and falling rocks. Her mouth, almost knitted together with wrinkles, relaxed, and she laughed hoarsely, remembering a time when she was happy, not a common occurrence in her life.

"My father wouldn't let us sing in the house, only in church." I wondered where she learned the words to "Little Brown Jug," which I'd often heard her sing:

Yo ho ho, you and me
Little brown jug, don't I love thee?

"But in the mountains, he didn't care," she continued. "We sang and ran and played games along the shore. It was so beautiful and birds trilled. I felt like a bird, warbling and hopping from rock to rock, hiding in the trees. We lived in a tent with a wood floor and Mama cooked. And then a rider galloped in to tell us storms had hit the highest mountains and more were coming. It was only early September but we hurried to leave."

She lay still for a bit. I knew if I interrupted, the strains of her story might fade.

"Father hitched up the horses to our big wagon. We packed it full of the summer leavings and our clothes as fast as we could go. 'Hurry. Hurry.' I left my favorite shirt-waist and was scolded later. We climbed into the back of the wagon—Grover, Almia, Apal, and me. Waldo was still small and sat with Mama in front next to Father."

These names were familiar to me. I had known Aunt Almia and Aunt Apal. The others were faces that stared out from family albums. Whenever Grandmother Elsie or my mother pulled the photos out, I felt as if I were seeing living proof of the begats in Genesis —a sameness of language translated into a lineage of square shoulders, hawk faces, and largely humorless visages. No receding chins, no shifty eyes. Even the blue of my family's eyes stare out through the years in challenge, smoky gray in white skin above black suits and black dresses.

"With his whip cracking, Father urged the horses on and we climbed up and up the mountain road—so narrow I was afraid we would fall off and tumble over and over into the river below. My teeth rattled as we bumped along. Then Father jerked us to a stop. A rock slide blocked our way and it was beginning to snow!" Her voice quavered, not with age as it sometimes did, but with excitement. "We couldn't go back. We could hardly go ahead, but Father decided to press forward. He said we'd be trapped for the winter and starve to death if we did not. We rocked from back to front and side to side. My bones shook and cracked." Her voice grew even stronger as she rocked herself on her hospital pillow. "Almia and Apal and I held each other to keep from being bounced out. We finally made it to the other side of the rocks. Right behind us, snow gobbled up the road. We were so cold, but we made our way home. I never went back to the mines." Her voice trailed and she plucked with long, bony hands at the rumpled sheets.

"Father took us all to church every Sunday. He said singing any-thing other than hymns to God was sinful." She lay quiet for a while. "Remember to sing when you're happy, Julie. And Mary, too. You have such beautiful voices." We did not, but my mother did.

I have traveled to Josephus Lakes, two glacier-scraped pockets of deep blue. In the rocks above the water, I found several square nails and the jumbled remains from blasting. My great-great-grand-father and my great-grandfather, both immigrants to Idaho from Missouri, did not find gold. My grand-uncle Grover tells in a family history of searching for a storied hidden sack of gold nuggets above the lakes, and finding nothing.

But the heritage my great-grandfather left me was worth more than a sack of gold: a love of Idaho, from the high hidden lakes of the River of No Return Wilderness to the sagebrush deserts around Hailey and the Silver Creek Preserve to the waters of the Selway and Lochsa rivers tumbling from the Bitterroot Mountains along the Montana-Idaho border to the forested mountains around Coeur d'Alene Lake and all of the mountain ranges of both southern and northern Idaho: Pioneer, Smokey, Boulder, Sawtooth, White Cloud, Bitterroot, Salmon River. The glories of Idaho contrast sharply with the ruined landscape around Kellogg, and yet, it is Kellogg and its residents who come back to me time and again in my memory.

* * *

Most of my friends' families came to Idaho from elsewhere. My family seemed always to be a part of Idaho, and I am in the fifth generation to live here. My great-great-grandfather Isaac Pfost trav-eled to southern Idaho in a covered wagon in 1878. He had signed a note for a friend in Missouri who followed the gold rush to Califor-nia and never returned. Paying the debt broke Isaac, so he headed west himself to find a new and better life, but the only work to be had was cutting cords of wood and selling them in the settlement of Boise City. My great-grandfather, Martin Burns, left Missouri, too, to earn money to save his father's farm. He also settled in Boise City, finding work as a freighter, and then laboring in the lead and silver mines around Hailey and Ketchum. In 1885, at the age of thirty-two, he married Isaac's daughter Mollie, a girl of eighteen. Their first home was in the mining town of Ketchum. Later they homesteaded desert claims in an area referred to as The Valley near what is now Meridian, Idaho, outside of Boise.

Isaac and his son-in-law, Martin, both mined for lead and gold in the Seafoam mining area in the mountains to the north and west of Ketchum. Summers, Martin took his whole family, including my grandmother Elsie as a young girl, to the Josephus Lakes with him. He never struck a fortune in gold, but finally found enough to enable him to buy a store in Meridian, selling hard goods as Burns & Co.

Grandmother Elsie loved to sing and "Little Brown Jug" was one of her favorites, although she rarely if ever touched anything alcoholic. She was born at the Valley place, a small rented farm, where her mother delivered without benefit of doctor, midwife, husband, or even neighbor. At sixteen, Elsie attended the University of Idaho. When she sent home a photograph of herself in a dress with off-the-shoulder sleeves, her father pulled her out and sent her to college at Albion Normal. Upon graduation she taught grade school in Cambridge, Idaho. She married my Grandfather Frank, the stationmaster of the Cambridge depot.

Grandfather Frank, my mother's father, grew up on a farm in Wisconsin, along with brothers and sisters, cousins, aunts, uncles, and parents, an extended German family that still spoke the home country language. He left public school after the eighth grade and entered telegraphy school, enabling him to get his first job with the railroad in Omaha. Over the years, he advanced from railroad agent—handling freight, selling tickets, cleaning up—to station agent for Cambridge, Parma, Twin Falls, and Pocatello, and then to regional transportation director, regional station master, and finally to head of all the Union Pacific Railroad depots in the West.

While my mother and her brother were still young, my grandmother began to accuse my grandfather of love affairs, trysts with the neighbor lady in Pullman cars and with other women in hotels in Pocatello, Twin Falls, and in towns where he traveled with his railroad job. She imagined conspiracies between him and his lady loves to do my grandmother in. She "heard" them planning, talking, making love. The devil, she loudly exclaimed, was in my Grandfather Frank and his assorted satanish doings were killing her, causing her pain. Christian Science appealed to her, as did tablespoons of lime powder every day for her ailments, always caused, she insisted, by my grandfather's bad thoughts.

Two of Elsie's favorite pastimes were buying things at auctions and investing in land. After Elsie died, my mother cleaned out her closets and basement, which were filled with things: letters and birthday cards received over the years, monthly bills and tax statements; boxes filled with cotton and tissue paper; bottles of cologne and dusting powder canisters; pillows and quilts she'd sewn by hand along with scraps of silk, chenille, crepe, cotton, and wool; peacock feathers and goose down; costume jewelry; pink cut-glass lamps; shelves and shelves of canned goods dating back at least twenty years; jelly dishes by the dozen, lead crystal and pressed glass pitchers, and a full set of cobalt blue glasses for water, wine, aperitifs, and champagne. It took me many years to cadge these glasses from my mother.

Upright in stance and morals, broad-shouldered but slender, my grandmother was a beauty in her youth, with full lips and round pale eyes. A picture of my grandmother in her wedding dress is sepia-toned. But even the age of the photograph does not hide the small wisps of curly hair escaping the bonds of the satin bow at the back of her slender neck. The lace and lawn materials hang gracefully from a fashionable wasp waist and womanly hips. An Eve ripe for life, ready for love.

As she aged, lines etched her face, pursing her mouth in wrinkles, and unhappiness seeped from her eyes. She crimped her hair in curls and dyed away the gray. Her large hands and feet seemed larger, but she did not shrink as many women do in old age. When her stomach aches finally were diagnosed as cancer, it was too late to cut it out.

A fiftieth-anniversary invitation created by my mother contained photos of my grandparents when they were young. My grandfather's dark, stern, square-jawed handsomeness explained my grandmother's attraction to him, even though he was unread and rough-spoken in the early years. When I knew him as a child, he always wore a dark suit with a vest and a watch chain, and a gray felt hat. By his forties, he resembled Harry Truman and often told stories of being confused with the former president when traveling on railroad duties. After he retired, which would have been in the 1950s, he visited us frequently, sometimes staying a month at a time, to "give him a rest" from my grandmother, my mother said.

No one believed Frank was unfaithful to Elsie. Not my mother or my uncle and none of the children. We saw a short, bald man with a paunch and steel-rimmed eyeglasses and couldn't understand why she accused him. Perhaps Elsie still saw the handsome man he had been when she married him.

Fragments of letters from Frank showed up in some of Elsie's treasure trove, always with endearments sprinkled in between news of his travels and sending shirts home to clean, along with concerns about how she was getting by with their children and her housekeeping money.

It is difficult for me to imagine how they lived with each other, although I saw them together every August in Boise and McCall. She cooked in a hot kitchen while dressed in a slip and rolled-down stockings. He listened to baseball and walked his dog Jack. She raised boysenberries and chickens and tended a garden with her sister Apal, growing vegetables and fruit. He irrigated and mowed the lawn, tied up the berries, wrote letters to my mother and to us children and, for a while, raised a horse. He wore his undershirt in the summertime, with his suspender straps hanging from his waist. He told us railroad stories about train wrecks and bandits with guns.

On the beach of Payette Lake in McCall, Idaho, where we visited each summer, he sat in the shade wearing his gray hat and undershirt, slacks and suspenders, carving bark playthings for the girl cousins—plates, cups, knives, spoons. He played endless games of Monopoly and pinochle (which we had all learned from my grandmother) with us children, and cribbage with my mother. In the evenings, he listened to baseball, hunched over by the cathedral-style radio. Whenever I hear a broadcast of a game now, the rustle of the audience, the crack of the bat, the announcer reporting a "hiiiigh pop fly," I see my grandfather still.

* * *

My father's family came from Pennsylvania and Virginia and Tennessee, a scattered, fragmented heritage, to settle near Spokane, Washington, in the late 1800s. My father's mother, Grandma Hattie, said *her* mother deserted her father, and so he came west with the children, including Hattie. She told of bringing the cows in from the hills to milk, and her voice and grammar reflected her country and southern background. My mother refers to it as vulgar speech. "I'd never heard such language until I met Glen's mother. I'd never heard anyone say 'pee' before. And she said it all the time!"

Grandma Hattie, whom we saw much more frequently than Elsie because Spokane was only sixty miles away from Kellogg, was a favorite with me most of the time. Her creamy skin barely lined, a result she said of her English and Irish heritage, tightly curled hair, a comfortable body, old-lady shoes, and the smell of Pond's cold

cream—those are my images of her. She was a source of contradic-
tions: ghost stories about youngsters getting lost in caves and only
their bones being found, endearments to us, accusations to Grandpa Glen, first secrets of sex (it was from Grandma Hattie that I
learned about a man's erection), ample lap, presents in white boxes
with colored ribbons always wrapped twice around, scoldings
about keeping warm and wearing a hat, put-upon-isms, welcoming
arms, and name-calling.

She took care of us when my parents traveled, and only as I grew
older did I object, more on grounds that we could take care of
ourselves than any dislike. Having my father (her son) away was
always a relief. When my face bloomed with blackheads, white-
heads, and pimples, I noticed her skin, "peaches and cream" she
called it. If only I'd wash more, she promised, all those spots would
go away. After piano lessons in Spokane we visited her house, filled
with glass and china figurines that caught the evening light, reflecting prisms on the walls, porcelain birds and shepherdesses,
fuzzy carpets and thin towels, white sparkling kitchen and the
comfortable presence of my grandfather, the two of them always
sniping. But she also called him "honey." "Honey, water the lawn."
"Honey, turn up the heat." Fried chicken, chicken-fried steak, silky
mashed potatoes and white gravy, and overcooked peas awaited us.
What smelled even better than food frying in butter and Crisco?
Large, dark molasses cookies, my favorite, and apple pie fresh from
the oven, syrupy, slightly tart. Sweet and tart—that was Grandma
Hattie.

My father's father, Grandpa Glen, sold used cars for a living.
Taunts about used-car salesmen never made sense to me, as I knew
my grandfather as a friendly, sweet, and honest man, putting up
with sharp, daily criticism from my grandmother. He reflected his
German heritage: large nose, dark brown hair that turned gray only
in his late seventies, a huge stomach.

My father was an only child. His mother worked in a book binding company as a bindery "girl." After school, my future father started the fire and dinner; when his mother arrived home, she finished preparations. During World War II, Grandpa Glen worked at Pacific Fruit Company, where he could make more money for my father's schooling, and then he returned to car sales. Because neither Hattie nor Glen had any more than a grammar school education, they were determined their son would go to college.

Music became a passion of my father's life, beginning at an early age. By the time he was twelve years old, he played in a dance band, first on a banjo and then on the drums. Gonzaga, a Jesuit college in Spokane, offered my father a music scholarship. His parents disapproved of Roman Catholics and wouldn't let him attend. Instead, he entered the University of Idaho at the same time my mother did. Rather than studying music, he began the pre-med program, in part because several fraternity brothers were enrolled. If they could do it, he figured, so could he.

My parents met at the University of Idaho, where my mother studied art and my father directed his own college dance band. He played the drums, the banjo, the piano, and chummed with the other band members, many of whom were fraternity brothers. My mother's fondest memories, ones she relives through a four-inch-thick souvenir album of dance cards and clippings, are of her college days and her successes in her sorority, her social life, her academics and art. She was engaged first to one of the other band members and then to my father. Both, she avowed, were the best musicians, the best dancers.

During his sophomore year, my father took the opportunity to join a dance band on a cruise ship to the Philippines. Upon his return to school, his musicians' union fined him for playing with a nonunion band on the ship. To earn out the fine, the union found him a summer job in Kellogg, Idaho, playing with fraternity brothers at the Corner Club, a dance and poker den underneath the corner drugstore. Kellogg was a wide-open, Wild West town, with gambling, drinking, brothels, good times. It appealed greatly to my father.

While my mother headed to the University of Iowa to study painting in graduate school, my father drummed, gambled with buddies, played the slot machines, and drank his way through a northern Idaho gig. Then he returned to finish his senior year at Idaho.

Armed with her master's degree and the knowledge that she had exhibited artwork at the New York World's Fair in 1939, my mother married my father shortly before he entered medical school at the University of Chicago. My brother was born in 1940.

Mother told me this story about their first Christmas in Chicago: "Your dad sold blood for twenty-five dollars. It was a way for medical students to make money if needed. He bought me the two-volume notebooks by Leonardo da Vinci that I still have, and a blue jacket from Marshall Field's that I wore out many years ago. I thought it was one of the nicest things he ever did. You know, twenty-five dollars in 1939 was a lot of money, especially considering the fit he had when I spent four dollars for a bed pillow." Although a successful and good medical student, my father continued to gamble and drink.

After an internship in Denver, where I was born, my father served in the last year of World War II, operating in an army hospital near Cherbourg, France. When he was discharged from the service at Missoula, Montana, where my sister was born in 1946, he turned down an offer to purchase a thriving medical practice there and headed for Kellogg, a place of fond memories from his summer of music, a mining town of over six thousand people. Kellogg needed good doctors and offered a young physician an opportunity to begin practice in unfettered, friendly surroundings.

Dad couldn't resist the lure. My mother had no choice. She thought Kellogg was dreary and ugly. He assured her they would leave after five years. That never happened.

8
When the Slot Machines Went Out

My mother had visited Kellogg while going to college in Moscow. Her view was entirely different from my father's. "I arrived in the town late at night," she said. "In the morning when I awoke and looked out the window, a mountain arose right from the backyard. It looked almost straight up. Because I came from flat country, southern Idaho, I was almost overwhelmed. Main Street to the business district was all downhill. The sidewalks were narrow. I was accustomed to Twin Falls, a town that was well planned, with wide streets all paved, regular blocks and well-cared-for yards and grass in the parking strips. Kellogg, a mining town, had grown like Topsy over the available space and some not-so-available space without much coordination. There were roads up to the houses built on the hills. Division Street rambled up the gulch into and through Wardner. There was little order to the blocks. The downtown was two streets—Main and McKinley. The whole town was strange!"

In 1946, my father opened his one-man practice in the late fall. He needed examining tables, medical instruments, an X-ray machine, all the accoutrements of medical practice, for his new office. One of his first patients was Dixie, the local madam, who paid cash for all services to herself and her "girls." She financed the tools of his trade. In the beginning, although Kellogg had its own hospital, named Wardner Hospital after a predecessor in the Milo Gulch area, owned by the Bunker Hill Company, he sent patients to the Sisters of Providence Hospital in Wallace, a particularly ironic situation, given the kinds of patients he treated. He hospitalized Dixie there for an operation and short stay. When she recovered and left the hospital, she forgot a money stash she had hidden under the mattress. The Sisters returned it to her. The notorious madam swore the Sisters were nicer to her than anyone ever had been. My only memories of the nuns were black robes, heavy silver crosses, and white wimples bearing chocolate ice cream cones from the kitchen.

Dad's first office was on the second floor of the Weber Bank, an institution homegrown in the early mining camp days. An enterprising individual had set up shop in the late 1800s inside a dry goods store, taking deposits of cash from the miners. At first, the new banker just held the money, charging a fee for keeping it in a large black safe with a combination lock. Curlicue gold lettering, outlined in silver, swirled grandly on the outside: Weber's Deposit Company. Then the entrepreneur loaned money, paid and earned interest, charged additional fees, and eventually the big black steel safe became a big black marble building in Kellogg.

Even as a new doctor, my father was busy. He made two trips a day to Providence Hospital in Wallace, and he made house calls, sometimes miles out of town to one of the gulches or up the North Fork of the Coeur d'Alene River. Sixteen-hour days were commonplace, and the only time he was home was for dinner and later to sleep awhile. That never changed. Dad was gone most of the time. All the doctoring for our family came from my mother, unless we were seriously ill. She opened the medicine cabinet, a huge cupboard filled with samples of every kind of medicine, selected one for whatever ailed us, and dispensed it to us. Presumably, she checked with Dad, but we thought of her as "our" doctor.

Women would call at nights and on weekends about their children. One said to my mother on an evening when he was out making a call, "But my child has a temperature of 101!" One of us had a temperature of 104, and she didn't know where he was or when he would be home. Another caller was one whose voice she came to recognize as Dixie's. It was low-pitched with a gravelly quality.

There were only two other doctors in town and they were associated with the Wardner Hospital. They sometimes employed young doctors who never seemed to stay. Before long, they asked my father to join their practice. Soon he, too, sent his patients to the company hospital.

The town was "wide open," just as he remembered it from his college days and as Dee and Dora Tatham described it. Slot machines and card games could be found in nearly every bar, which far outnumbered the churches. A grocery store, a gas station, and a shoe shop had slots. Houses of prostitution lined up along Railroad Avenue, and during the time gambling was still legal, one, two or three women sold themselves upstairs in the bars, sometimes in the McConnell Hotel or above an automobile garage or behind a grocery store. Even after gambling ended, the brothels stayed.

As the town grew, some of the wildness diminished. Legal gambling ended, and the small-time prostitutes either left or joined the larger houses. When slots became illegal, December 31, 1953, an unusual ceremony was held.

That day the chief called Chuck Biotti, who worked as a policeman as well as a miner. "He says, 'Chuck, I want you up at the station. We're gonna patrol the Union Legion tonight. Put your uniform on. At midnight tonight is when the slot machines are going to be outlawed.'"

Chuck headed to the Union Legion hall, where every room held slot machines—seventy-five or a hundred of them. "Someone got a casket from the mortician," he said, "and they got a slot machine in it and took the lid off. Six fellows took the casket out of the building. They were singing a funeral song on the way out, and they put it in the truck. I don't know what they did with it."

I did. It went into our basement.

"When the slot machines left Kellogg, the city lost $80,000 a year," Chuck said. "You had to buy a license for each machine. The state got a cut. The county got a cut. And whatever came out of the back of the slot machine goes to whoever has the license on it." A nickel machine license cost $250, a dime machine $500, and a dollar machine $1,000 a year.

Even without the slot machines, people still gambled in card games, pull-tabs, and dice in the back rooms of bars and clubs, and not until the late 1980s did law enforcement officials take any major action against gambling and prostitution. My father belonged to a group—the Jesters—who regularly met and played high stakes cards. He lost a lot of money that way. Unlike other fathers I knew, my father didn't hunt, fish, golf, ski, or follow politics. His hobbies were working, drinking, playing music, and gambling. Perhaps no other town could have accommodated him as well as Kellogg.

My father was the clichéd tall, dark, and handsome man with startling blue eyes. My mother was petite, also dark-haired, deep-blue-eyed, and lovely. They made an attractive couple on the dance floor—young, reasonably athletic, vibrant, devoted. The picture often did not reflect the reality, perhaps in some of the same ways that the picture of a prosperous town did not always reflect the dangerous work underground and the chemicals and poisons swirling into the air from the smelting processes.

* * *

Our neighborhoods could have been any small town in America, *Leave It to Beaver* kinds of places, except for the fact that there were no trees on the sidehills. At our ages, none of us thought to wonder why they were bare. *Our* trees—the maples—turned gold and red in the fall and furnished leaves for class projects. A cemetery covered the hilltop at one end of town, near a house where we lived when I was in the first grade. If there were deaths of miners from accidents or miners' consumption, this was not something we knew about. We only knew the cemetery was spooky and no one wanted to be caught in it at night.

We played outside winter and summer, sledding down an alleyway behind the house, stacked three or four to a sled to make us go faster, and roaming from yard to yard in the summer. Outside our front door, where flowers were supposed to be planted, horsetails grew. My brother convinced me they were tiger tails and one day we would be attacked and eaten up.

Chuck Biotti's family lived across the street. His daughter Diane was a good friend. Chuck was gone all day and half the night, as my father was, and her mother, Elaine, sewed. All the satin and net costumes for the dance programs, organdy and lace and lawn gowns for weddings and proms, she designed and fashioned. She tailored and tucked, took in and let out suits and dresses for women in town. Diane's house was filled with her mother's ample, warm self and also with pattern pieces, lengths of textured materials in bright blues, greens, red and pinks, thread spools, zipper parts, and tape measures. Over the years, I visited often because Elaine was a willing listener with good advice and a caring heart. She nodded her head, straight pins in her mouth, the sewing machine riddling along a seam, then stopped to remove the pins and talk and gossip with me, just as if I were an adult. Diane's father, Chuck, stood tall and slender in his police uniform. Policing was a second job when he finished work at the Bunker Hill each day. The whole family's black hair and dark brown eyes reflected their Italian heritage.

The house where we lived longest was on McKinley Avenue, one of five major streets in the town. This street began uptown, intersected Main, and then was a straight shot west past a dozen bars, a cafe, two dress shops, a hardware store and other small businesses, the YMCA, the football stadium, and many houses, including ours, all the way to the Bunker Hill office building, mine entrance, mill, rockhouse, crushing plant. It continued past the area where families from Oklahoma and Arkansas lived, to Smelter Heights, a total distance of perhaps a mile-and-a-half, almost as long as the mine was deep. Miners going to and from work passed our house in shifts every day, sometimes walking with lunch buckets, more often riding in cars forming a steady stream of headlights. The mine entrance was a long block from my front door.

This neighborhood was halfway between uptown and Smelter Heights with maple trees shading the houses and the hospital, the hospital parking lot, several vacant lots, and the Bunker Hill Staff House. At the end of the parking lot was a drop-off to mud and sand flats, the railroad tracks, and the city park. The area between the city park, where we learned to swim, and the mine buildings was a no-man's land—red earth with a trickling creek and occasional cattails, handy missiles in our neighborhood battles.

We lived on the east side of the hospital; another doctor's family lived on the west side, with still another doctor across the street. Many of the houses on McKinley belonged to the Bunker Hill Company, which rented them to us and provided heat and water. The "company town" aspect of Kellogg wasn't limited to the miners. My father's livelihood depended on the mines, too.

Dozens of canaries lived in the basement of one of the doctor's houses. The smells of ammonia and poop permeated their house. There was a constant rustle in the doctor's basement, bird claws gripping perches, scratching paper, traversing wire cage tops and sides, cracking pellets of food. The birds trilled and sang in cages, one on top of another, row after row. No sun. No fresh air. No insects or clouds or fresh water. On the other hand, if they had been freed, they would have died of lead poisoning. Only robins lived in Kellogg.

My sister and I surely resembled birds. We had thin arms and legs, in my case knock-kneed, thin chests and thin faces and thin hair. What was it? The air or water? But other girls in the neighborhood were almost pudgy.

Smelter Heights, at the west end of McKinley, contained large brick and colonial-style homes for the top mine managers and officers. Behind them, the smelter belched smoke and steam into Deadwood Gulch and across the valley. Nearby in Government Gulch, the zinc plant did the same. More houses lined the road across from this plant. Down the hill from the Heights was Smelterville, named for obvious reasons, one of which was the slag mountain. An impoundment area west of town held the tailings ponds. We roller skated at a rink in Smelterville and ice skated on the sloughs beyond the tailings. Lead Creek, always flowing mush-gray and thick, wound its way through Sunnyside, the area of Kellogg near the river, past a small but functional airport, past Smelterville, and past the slough, carrying its lead, arsenic, and other wastes through the valleys in the Panhandle, and on to Coeur d'Alene Lake.

Haystack Peak, named for its shape, rose out of the vacant field behind our house and the hospital. Like the other low mountains around the town, it grew no trees. But unlike most of the others, it was green in spring and summer with snowberry, alder bushes, and sweet-smelling syringa.

We lived in the outdoors whenever we could, and one of our activities was playing Indians on Haystack Peak. A road cut across it, heading up from the alley behind our house to an abandoned mine, the Last Chance, considerably higher than the entrance to the Bunker Hill workings at the end of our block. We used the first part of the road to sled down in winter and to reach our Indian villages in spring and summer. We spent hours building our huts, making up rules, deciding relationships.

The ground smelled of dirt and rotting leaves—a deep earthy smell, damp and thick. We pulled out slender branches of the alder and syringa, cutting thick ones, to make closely barred walls for our huts. We used vines as twine to hold them together and placed leafy branches over the tops to protect us from rain. We matted grass for our floors, tramped paths from one hut to the next.

None of the girls could be braves. "Squaw" designated all of us. Our mothers, too, fit that role. Squaw—helpmate. Our mothers were the ones with whom we lived and talked, who cooked, cleaned, nurtured and cared for us, helped with homework, and most were ever-present. Our fathers were strangers, visitors in our houses at night, accompanying families on vacations, meting out punishments. Those were the roles we accepted and the ones we played in our games.

At the back of the hospital, large garbage cans lined the alley, as well as a garbage pile. All sorts of medicine vials, glass containers, and interesting stuff like rubber tubes, gauze, hypodermic syringes (no needles) found their way into our Indian camp (but not the bottles with what looked like organs and even fetuses in them) to serve as trading goods should we ever meet other tribes who wished to trade. Straw grass and dandelion seed balls flourished in the field behind the hospital, across the alley from its garbage heap.

So did our carnival. At my brother's direction, two of his friends cleared rocks and flattened the grass. Three of us girls rigged booths with sheets and cardboard. We cooked Rice Krispies, gooey with marshmallows, in our mothers' kitchens and mixed lime Kool-Aid. All six of us collected prizes: lead soldiers, stuffed animals, small lead-cast jackasses (the souvenir of choice for visitors to Kellogg, commemorating the way the initial silver strike was found), tiny cars and plastic dolls, and then we blew up red, yellow, and green balloons.

Across the top of a whiskey barrel painted blue and pink, my brother drove a thick spike through a long, wide plank. *Wham, wham*, like a pile driver. He stood next to the barrel, wearing his cape and tall hat, and turned the plank, spinning two riders around.

I dressed like a gypsy with clanking gold charm bracelets, a bandanna on my head, and watermelon-red lipstick, to tell fortunes with a black eight ball: "Your luck will turn." "The answer is no." "Not this time." "Wait for next year."

Fish at the pond, we called. Five cents! Toss a dime into a bottle! Win prizes! Kool-Aid, three cents! A quarter to ride the plank! Three darts for ten cents! Fortunes for a nickel! Kids flocked in, shouting with success, moaning with misses. Nickels and dimes and quarters jingled. Windows of the hospital stared down.

Then my father came out, still wearing his green surgery clothes and the funny knit cap on his head. He stalked up to my brother: "Was this your idea?"

"We're making money," he said.

"You're waking patients." My father, his hand white and hard, slapped our ride. "You'll hurt someone." He pointed to the dime-toss. "Where did you get the medicine bottles?"

My brother glanced toward the garbage and said nothing.

"How could you be so stupid?" My father raised his arm and then stopped. Without looking back, he stomped into the hospital. The door closed behind him, a *whoooosssssshhhhh* across the silent field.

*   *   *

In my growing-up years, I knew the mine was just beyond our house and Bunker Hill employed most of the men in the town, but I didn't think about it, except perhaps in terms of whose father worked where and money flowing in and out of town. I also knew that my friends' last names and sometimes nicknames, like Bohunk, reflected roots in different parts of the world.

The *Kellogg Evening News* reported daily on the prices of metals, the deepening of shafts, the coming and going of mine officials, the planning for new facilities such as the acid plant or additional waste processes like the heightening of dirt walls of the tailings ponds, and, occasionally, mine accidents or deaths. Our focus was on news important to us: ski races in which my brother and I participated, Little League baseball reports, YMCA activities such as Tri-Hi-Y for girls and Hi-Y for boys, basketball and football scores, descriptions of weddings, dances, and even birthday parties, and club reports in which my mother's name might be mentioned.

Few non-miners visited the mines or processing plants. No one conducted tours for schoolchildren to explain how the ores were mined or even what they looked like or what supported all of us. No one taught geology at school; few talked about our "company town." And yet the mines were as much a part of our existence as the high school across the valley, Densow's (later Damiano's) Drug, Joe & Henry's bar and pool room, or the law office where I worked after school and on Saturdays. Miners streamed by our house morning and afternoon. My father doctored them and other townspeople alike. The slag heap, the tailings ponds, the smelter smoke, all seemed normal aspects of our lives. The shift sirens marked the passage of our days. The lights of the rockhouse, mill, and smelter burned day and night.

Much closer to me was the hospital next door.

9

How's Your Body? I

The three-storied clapboard hospital loomed over our house. Twelve steps led to the front veranda and door, and in the 1950s when I was young, it was the largest wood building in town, built like a southern plantation with columns and wide porches on each level.

No grass grew in the narrow passageway between the two wood structures, perhaps ten feet wide with a sidewalk down the middle to the front yard from our back door. On fall afternoons, I raked leaves in our yard and the hospital yard. With a big enough stack, we neighborhood kids ran and jumped into them, scattering gold, yellow, and red on the brown grass. My sister and I and our girl friends designed leaf houses, using our rakes to outline with leaves a kitchen, living and bed rooms, porches, and dens. There we played with our dolls and assigned mother, father, and children roles to each other. At night, we built snow forts in winter or played kick-the-can in summer. If our games grew too noisy, one of the nurses stepped out on the veranda and asked us to quiet down.

My father doctored there, tending the miners who worked at the Bunker Hill Mine and their families and the rest of the town's residents. My older brother, my younger sister, and I chased through it like a second home. Out our back door, down three concrete steps, up wood steps to the side entrance and through the door into a green hallway, to call our father to dinner. I smelled ether and dodged the activity: nurses bustling in white dresses, starched caps, and white hose; patients draped with green sheets on gurneys being wheeled into the elevator; miners' wives waiting for news; other doctors passing from room to room; orderlies carrying bandages and medicines. Turn right, turn left along another hallway, down the steps to the clinic, past empty examining rooms—they always looked like torture chambers to me.

"Dinner's ready," I announced at my father's office door.

"Slow down," he said. "Wait a minute." A thin line of smoke from his Camel cigarette wafted up from the ashtray, overflowing with butts. His glass-topped, dark wood desk with two chairs in front, almost filled the small room. On the wall hung his diplomas from the University of Idaho and the University of Chicago Medical School, along with one of my mother's paintings of the smelter, smoke belching from a stack and the slag pile black in the foreground.

Paper piles covered his desk. He cradled a telephone between his neck and shoulder, getting in a last call, checking off a last form, writing a prescription in his unreadable scrawl. I plunked down in a chair, impatient, hungry.

I watched his hands. They were different at work than at home. At work they were patient hands, touching gently as if he had special senses in them that were hearing and seeing on their own, moving across an arm or down a back, feeling for pain in a stomach, at the neck, under the jaw. His eyes turned inward when his hands moved over a body, searching out pain and disease, nodules, strange pulses or wheezes, seeking the spot to fix, to cure.

At home his hands were large with fat finger pads and thick knuckles. They rapped a head, pulled hair, grasped a cocktail glass with ice and scotch and a splash of water. They broke a wine glass, spread peanut butter thick on bread, swiped grease on a plate with a biscuit, snapped fingers, pointed, accused. They rarely smacked—his words did that—and often shook.

When I was seven, I liked to walk down the halls with my father.

"How's your body?" he asked everyone he met, his patient or not.

"Hey, Doc," they answered.

A miner explained how his broken arm and torn skin and muscles had healed, showing him the scar, as if my father hadn't sewed it up himself. Four steps later, a woman stopped to tell him how her son was doing away at college and how much the scholarship from Bunker Hill had been, then asked about her prescription for arthritis.

"I'll call George at the drugstore, have him renew it."

A nurse conferred briefly about a patient. "Ward 4, second bed needs something else to ease the pain."

"Give him two more ccs of ——," he said, naming a pain killer that meant nothing to me. "I'll be back after dinner and I'll check on him then."

I grabbed his hand and danced around, tapping my feet on the linoleum floor. He ignored me until he had spoken to everyone who waved or stopped. Then out the back door of the "horse pistol" as he called it, and down the steps we hurried.

My father often wore clinic clothes all day—white cotton pants and shirt, or green after coming out of surgery, along with a funny little hat, a cotton-knit thing gathered at the top. Other days, he donned slacks and a shirt and tie and a white clinic jacket. A stethoscope, if it wasn't around his neck, drooped from the pocket. His shoes always seemed huge, his tread heavy; he was a big man with a fat stomach.

When we entered the kitchen, he danced my mother around and gave her a big noisy smooch, saying, "Hi honey! What's for chow tonight?" With luck, Mother hadn't cooked a new, exotic-for-Kellogg dish. Our family dinner hour was often uncomfortable enough without having to gag down curry, cabbage, stuffed green peppers, or creamed onions—dishes my father loved. Clean plates were the rule at our house. My brother, sister, and I sat, hoping for reprieve. We prayed the telephone would ring, calling my father back to the hospital. If it did, he'd take a last bite, grab his jacket and stethoscope, and leave. Then, with our mother's blessing, we would pick up our plates where we'd shoved congealing food back and forth for an hour and take them to the kitchen, released from purgatory.

*   *   *

The X-ray room was on the first floor of the hospital, along with a fluoroscope, that magic machine that showed bones in green and ignored skin altogether, just like the one at Hutton's Department Store. Were arms or legs broken? Did bone spurs grow on toes? Were vertebrae crushed or skulls fractured? Were shoes too wide, too short, too narrow? How much radiation did we get in those days?

A black table hunkered in the middle of the room. I know because my friend Diane had hurt herself skiing at a teen outing. We rode the bus home together and I went with her when she was wheeled in for X-rays. The nurse technician turned wheels, pushed levers, made Diane take off her ski pants and sit half naked on the cold glasslike top. I waited at the head of the table, out of the way.

The nurse stepped behind a heavy lead screen. "Hold it," she ordered. *Whir, whir, click.* "Okay, you can move." Then she realized I was still there. "Julie, you can't stay in here while I x-ray. Wait outside." Diane looked at me with huge dark eyes, brown like her Italian father's.

The following summer, my father called me late one night from the hospital, saying, "Come to the X-ray room." He needed my help. I was a teenager and not inclined to help anyone, but arguing with him was not something I did lightly. I could never predict his reaction.

On the table lay one of my friends from school, his head bloodied and with white gauze wrapped around it, holding a large pad over his eye. Tears tracked his face. "Hi, Julie," he said, his voice quavering. My father readied the machine, inserting into a holder the square black glass upon which the X-ray image would be reflected.

"Hi." What was I supposed to do? All the blood and bandages made me feel queasy.

"Hold his hand, Julie. See if you can get him to sit still. I need X-rays of his skull. He lit a cherry bomb, dropped it in a bottle and blew it up."

While he situated my friend on the table, I held the boy's hand, pretending I was a gypsy, a part I'd played at Halloween. I opened his palm, still black with gunpowder, and traced the lines of his hand with my finger, telling him his life line was long and his heart line strong. He must be in love with someone. I questioned the steadiness of a line I called his intellectual definer and said he must study harder in school. When my father said, "Hold your breath and don't move," we both sucked in and held still as we could.

Whir, click click. My friend's skull was all right, but he had to have a glass eye. I remember how blue it was.

10

We're Giving You the Special Today

My father—Doc Whitesel to nearly everyone—took care of the miners. Many years later, when I interviewed several of his former patients, I found it hard to understand what they meant when they spoke of stopes, drifts, chutes, and drills. Virl, a retired hoistman, said he would take me to the Bunker. Then I could see for myself what a mine was like.

The November morning in 1990 was still dark when my guide opened the "dry" room, the miners' changing area, and found diggers, hardhat, lamp, and battery pack for my trip into the mine. Suited up, I felt as if I were heading off to do battle. The metal hardhat let me feel cocky, gave me a sense of invulnerability. Its lamp and the battery pack on the belt around my waist assured me I would have light wherever I walked. Rubber boots, only a couple of sizes too large for my feet, would protect me from mud, water, slipping, sliding, falling. I looked like a miner, one used to assaulting the rocks day after day and year after year, in the one-piece digger coverall with sleeves rolled up to my size and pants tucked into my boots.

I tried to forget that scuba diving lessons had sent me away crying from claustrophobia, that a high bluff or even a balcony has tempted me to jump off, and that a dark room suffocates me. Did I think my fear of closed, dark, and high places would leave me when I entered a mountain and traveled down to the workings of the Bunker Hill Mine in Kellogg, Idaho?

It was the self-rescue kit that almost undid me.

"What is that for?" I asked when fitted with a metal canister slightly wider than a small thermos onto my belt. Virl had been a friend and patient of my father's and has helped my widowed mother with odd jobs. In his late sixties then, Virl had wide shoulders, a barely lined face, a steady voice that was always on the edge of laughter. Only his curly steel-gray hair gave away his age. He would have fit any line-up for handsome men. And at the time, he still worked nearly every day, carpentering or laboring for neighbors and friends.

"Rules. We all have to wear 'em. Ever since the Sunshine fire."

The underground fire at the Sunshine Mine near Kellogg killed ninety-one men in 1972.

"But what does it do?"

"Damned if I know." A large laugh. "Nah. It lets you breathe when the air is full of smoke. Probably good for about fifteen minutes." Another jolly laugh. "Don't worry. We won't let anything happen to Doc Whitesel's daughter." He didn't offer to show me how to use the kit, and I didn't want to sound like a sissy, so I laughed, too. Then he leaned close and pretended to whisper: "Just don't tell anyone you're a lawyer. They'll think you're a spy for them EPA people."

"Today I'm a writer," I said, feeling self-conscious using that label. Although I had left Kellogg years before to attend college and then law school in Seattle, Washington, this trip into the mine marked a return to research the area for my writing of short stories and novels. I didn't want the miners' stories to disappear along with the shutdown of most of the mines in northern Idaho. Virl offered to show me what he had tried to tell me about, and I was fortunate that the Bunker mine had reopened, if only briefly.

Out into the cold air we went. The man-train, reminding me of a

Disneyland ride grown ancient, waited on the rails. Eight yellow cars, each about the size of half an elevator cage, with an electric engine at the back end and a trolley wire overhead. Another train with a shark's mouth painted on the front engine rested on the tracks a hundred yards behind.

"What's that one for?"

"Ore-train."

We climbed into a man-train car and sat across from each other, our knees almost touching. From his pocket, Virl pulled a cardboard box and handed it to me. The car jerked forward and we were on our way. We rumbled from the dark morning into the black tunnel under the sign "Kellogg Tunnel—1893–1902." The sound reverberated off the walls and through me. Virl twisted the ends of two yellow rubber pieces about the size of a large pill and put them in his ears. I took mine from the little box and did the same. Would we hear dynamite explode?

He leaned close and shouted. "We go two miles, then switch to the Number Two hoist. Wait till you see the cable on that sucker! Then," he said, and held his hand at a steep angle, "down." My stomach dropped at the same angle.

To keep my mind off cave-ins, broken cables, throwing up, or crying, I watched the dripping walls pass by, faintly illuminated by the train's headlight. Pipes, fat cables, and thin wires stretched along the sides. Sometimes the water disappeared and rocks or chunky dirt accompanied us. Virl shouted from time to time, but I couldn't hear most of what he said. "...siding." Or "...9 Level." Or "...stuck once."

The train slowed and we entered a huge room carved out of rock, brightly lit, perhaps two stories high and half as big as the gymnasium at the high school. We climbed out of our car and removed our earplugs. Several men sauntered by and others sat at a big picnic table. In the middle of the room was a metal shed high off the ground. A cable extended down to a large square hole in the ground and disappeared.

"That's where I worked substitute the last seven years before I retired. Come on over. This shaft is for the ore-skip. You'll go down a different one, but you should meet the kinda guy you gotta trust."

We climbed the stairs and I met the hoistman. His giant hand enclosed mine and squeezed. "Ever been down before?"

I shook my head. He and Virl talked mining talk for a few minutes while I studied the hoist shed. A big dial with numbers on it from one to twenty-seven. What looked like a gearshift handle and, I presumed, a brake. The metal was shiny with wear. How much wear? A huge cable drum and machinery stood behind the shed. Then, amidst a couple of nude pinup photos from magazines and a beach picture, I noticed a newspaper clipping pasted on the wall. "Earthquakes More Frequent Underground." And another: "Fault under Haystack Slipping." Haystack Peak was the bald hill behind my old house.

More headlines on more clippings told brief, tragic stories:

"91 Men Die in Sunshine Fire."
"Bolivian Cave-In Kills 20."
"All Hope Gone after Cable Breaks."

Because the hoistman in the Sunshine Mine died from smoke inhalation, dozens of men were trapped underground. I stopped scanning the walls and concentrated on the present hoistman, a fellow of medium height, slender build, dark-framed glasses. I was glad his hands were big. Maybe that meant strong muscles to pull hard on that brake.

"See the cable?" Virl asked, as we climbed down again. "Know how they got it in here?"

I looked at the metal drum, bigger than the hoist shed itself, and compared it to the tunnel opening. Couldn't be done, I thought.

"They unwound it from outside and pulled the cable through the tunnel and then rewound it here. Two inches thick."

"How long did you work in the mine?"

"Thirty-four years. I did everything from muckin', haulin' ore, skip-tendin', and hoistin'. I liked that best. Get to sit on your butt most of the day." At the bottom of the stepladder, he said. "I got you another guide to take you to the stopes. I gotta see some old friends of mine."

A young man, black-bearded and dressed in a plaid flannel shirt, yellow hardhat, black pants and boots, came up to us.

"This here's James. He's a schoolteacher, but he likes minin' better." Virl slapped James on the shoulder. James shook my hand.

"I knew your dad. He was my folks' doctor." His grip was warm and strong and he didn't squeeze. "Ready?"

"As I'll ever be," I said. I followed him toward the opposite end of the room from which we had arrived. He talked as we walked into a dark tunnel and he showed me how to turn on my lamp. My own sword of light beamed into the deepening murk. I wondered if The Force were with me.

"You're on 9 Level. Maybe Virl told you. One Level is up at Wardner. We'll take a man-skip down to 10 Level, and then if you're real brave, I'll take you to the lowest level that's open."

The Bunker Hill had closed at the end of 1981, and had been reopened for limited work off and on since then, up to and beyond the time I went down in it.[5] I wondered if the long closure meant the walls might tumble in, if the big timbers I saw along the tunnel could rot out, if the cable would break, but most of all I worried about an earthquake. How old were those clippings?

We walked along side by side between railroad tracks. If I stretched my arms out, I couldn't reach either wall of the tunnel. James warned me not to touch the wire over our heads—it carried electricity for the trolley trains. A constant wind blew. My schoolteacher guide explained, "Air comes into the mine all the time, down ventilation shafts. Huge fans suck it in, create the wind.

Compressed air is pumped in to run the machines, the drills. The stench system is built into the air lines."

Because he was a teacher, I figured I could ask all the dumb questions I wanted to. "What's a stench system?"

"They use it to warn the men to get out. Smells like rotten eggs. If there's a fire or anything wrong, gas, whatever, they load the system with this smell. It means 'drop everything and get the hell out.'"

I sniffed. No rotten egg odor, only musty dirt and a slightly metallic smell, like that of an abandoned basement. Ahead of us, huge doors slammed open, and Jim motioned me to the side.

"Skip's coming. You might want to put your earplugs in again. Flatten against the wall."

I followed his instructions. A big engine rumbled our way and passed on the tracks. The driver waved and beeped his horn. Behind him, he hauled a flatcar filled with two-by-six timbers and coiled metal wire.

"Those doors keep the wind from building up to gale force," James said as we passed through them.

We came to another hoist area. "Here's where we go down. Most folks only get to visit the main hoist area—that's where the ore comes up. But we're giving you the special today." I was pretty sure it was because my father was Doc Whitesel. He'd been dead thirteen years, but the memory of him in town was still strong—as a caring physician, hard drinker, and musician playing drums on his nights off at the Sunshine Inn.

James pulled on a handle—two dings, pause, then two more. "We're just going to 10 Level. The first two dings call the skip, the second ding is for the level." A long narrow metal sled with wood perches wide enough for two men each came up from the hole in the ground, making only a small whine on the rails. Virl got it right—about a forty-five degree or higher angle down—steep. I took a deep breath. "Tell me what to do."

"Climb in and sit on one of those lips. Keep your hands inside or you'll lose one quick. Hang on to me if you need to. I'll tell the hoistman to let us down easy at first so you can get used to it." He left and came back, climbed in beside me, and I moved closer to him.

"During shift changeovers, these man-skips are filled from top to bottom, hold about twenty-two men. First in, first out, stopping at each level as they go down."

Slowly, we dropped. Huge timbers, maybe twelve-by-twelves, held up the mountain just above my head. I was glad I wasn't tall. The men must have to scrunch down. I studied the beams carefully, especially after I saw one that looked as if it had a break down the middle. I glanced over at James. He didn't seem concerned. Then the skip sped up. Had the cable broken? Again, my guide didn't seem concerned. We dropped rapidly, then slowed for 10 Level and stopped exactly at the collar or platform level. How did the hoistman know? My respect for Virl grew.

We climbed off and began to walk again, this time down a drift, the same thing as a tunnel, but it was enclosed inside the mountain with no entrance from the open air. My boots splatted in mud between the rails. Except for the *splat, splat*, our voices and the sound of the wind, the drift was quiet. Then *clatter, clatter, beep, beep, clatter, whoosh, slam!* Another skip on the rails.

"He must have a new horn," James shouted as the engine clattered by us, carrying a few timbers, cable, tools, and a lunch box.

We stopped at a small ell in the drift. My lamplight showed a narrow metal ladder disappearing straight down into a black hole.

"We'll climb down here into a stope where they're working. I'll go first, then you follow. Some of the rungs on the wood ladders are a little rotten so I'll warn you if you have to skip a step."

"But isn't that metal?"

"Yeah, but some of the others are wood."

"There's more than one?"

He nodded and appeared to be computing in his head. "Probably seven or eight, one after the other. Say, a hundred feet down or so."

A hundred feet! That was as deep as a ten-story building is tall.

"Is that the only way to get there?"

"Yup. It's about halfway, maybe a little more, between 10 Level and 11 Level. That's how we mine. We dig up from one level to the other, blast out rock, shove it down chutes to the lower level, where ore cars take it to the hoist and up." Jim swung onto the ladder and started down. I had to follow. My knees shook, butterflies crashed around inside me, my hands gripped the rungs like death. Down I went. After the first twenty rungs, my nerves calmed. The hole was narrow enough that falling wasn't really an option. I slipped once, though, and grabbed the ladder sides to wait until my trembling stopped.

"You okay?" James's voice sounded from the black well below me.

"I'm fine, thank you."

Finally, we reached bottom. In the light of our lamps, I could see three workmen twenty-five feet away in a large hollowed-out room, the stope. One man leaned on a drill while the other two consulted a map, laid out on top of a baby elephant-sized machine. Two of them were shirtless. The air was close and warm, slightly humid, and smelled of ozone. No rotten eggs.

James consulted with the men, discussing the best way to follow the vein. In the area where I stood, by the ladders ready to climb up at the first warning of a cave-in, timbers crisscrossed like Lincoln logs held up the ceiling. In one area, plywood covered the side walls and overhang. Tubes from the man-way, the shaft we'd climbed down, led to the drill, to the squarelike machine, and along the wall. I assumed they conducted air and electricity, maybe water, too. James motioned me closer and introduced me to the men, explaining the drill was a jackleg drill, the machine was a mucker, and they were drilling a round for dynamite—a circle of holes into which dynamite sticks and fuses would be stuffed and lit. The question was where to go next. He tapped the survey map they had been studying.

"How do you know where you're going?" I asked.

"You can see the white rock seam there," one of the miners said and pointed. "And then another one right there. All that in between is the vein."

"What keeps the roof from falling in?"

"Sets of timbers. Want to put one in?"

I laughed a little shakily. "You wouldn't want to stand under one I'd put in. What are those timbers, ten-by-ten? You must use a lot of wood in here."

"Several billion feet in this place. A lot."

"If you can imagine it," James said, "what you're standing on right now, is a set, one square upon another square, like blocks."

The miner added: "We mine a floor, then we go up. Once it's mined out, slurry is pumped back in to fill it up. Sand."

"This is the highest-grade rock in the mine," James said. "This is the gravy. It's probably worth $250 a ton. This brown here is sphalerite, the soft part. There's lead in it too."

"The stuff Gulf was mining before they shut it down would make this look like a low-grade stope," the miner named Paul said. "It was always black. I never seen such bodies of ore in my life. Lot of silver. Lot of lead." Gulf Resources closed the Bunker Hill in 1982, when it seemed to run out of the rich ore and the costs of environmental safeguard and cleanup grew too great.

The men talked again about where to drill. One of them said: "The more we pull out there, the more it caves in on top of us, and we don't have nothing to stand under."

Paul added: "It almost looks like a straight go-ahead here instead of a turn. Maybe a little bit left, if anything."

"Yeah, yeah," James said. "It should be hanging off to the right. The main structure runs back like this." He moved his finger along the survey map.

"We're going to have to bring the post in just a little tiny bit to get in there without disturbing the whole mountain. It just keeps falling if you disturb it."

Whole mountain? I stepped back toward the ladders.

They settled on a direction and, as if a movie director had yelled "Action!", work began.

The miner on the jackdrill turned it on and a sound like hammering on concrete poured forth. Another miner climbed the mucker and its high-pitched, ear-splitting hum, *RRRrrrrrrrrRRRR*, prompted me to plug my ears. Paul, the one who talked the most about where to drill, took a long steel bar and struck at the walls and ceiling, bringing down big chunks of rock, "barring down." James picked up and threw a rock to me. Although it was half the size of a baseball, its weight nearly pulled me over when I caught it.

"That's iron and sulphur. Part of the muck. We're after galena, lead." He picked up another chunk, about two fists in size and sparkling. It was too heavy for me to hold. "It's pretty dense," he said. "There's silver in with the lead. Maybe I can find a piece of gold." He poked around at the end of the stope.

"It all looks like shale," I said, remembering one of the rocks from my college geology class. I moved to the wall.

"You don't want to stand real close to that side," James said. "It'll probably come down when he starts to drill the next hole."

I stepped away immediately.

"This dark chocolate brown stuff is sphalerite, zinc sulphide. It's kind of hard to see in here because there's so much iron that blacks it out."

We left the stope by climbing back up and then walked down another drift. Except for the beams from our lights, all was black, a dense emptiness. If our lamps went out, we'd be stuck. A loud fan hummed, although none was in sight. We reached a peg board.

"Tag board here. Each number is for a different stope. If there's a crew in the stope, they'll have a tag hanging here. Then when everybody is out of all the stopes, they'll start wiring in. Here's a set of wires for one stope." He pointed to a scramble of colored wires—black, green, blue, yellow. "Here's another, and another. They string different wires to different areas. The blasting box has flashlight batteries in it. Only needs a spark to set it off."

Then we walked to a small room off the drift, the explosives area. On the wall hung yellow fuse line in coils. James handed me small vials. "These are ammonia nitrate and fuel oil. If you squeeze one, your hands get oily. When they explode, all this vaporizes and then it makes a lot of gas and the gas expands and breaks the rock." He picked up a handful of pink Styrofoam balls. "This makes it a lighter explosive." A skip rumbled by. Another horn blew. "New horn. Everybody's got to try it out."

James picked up a yellow coil. "This is detonator cord, used to initiate the caps. That's the first thing that goes, the detonator cord. It burns at the rate of eight thousand feet per second, so it's instantaneous, and we use it to set off these." He handed me one. "Detonator caps." I couldn't hand it back fast enough. "They all have numbers. This is a *five*. It goes off in 1.4 seconds from the time it gets the impulse." He explained how holes were drilled in the rock, beginning in the middle and widening out. The rounds could be thirty-six holes, each the depth of the drill at five or six feet, or maybe twenty-four holes, even as low as fifteen holes, depending on how the "powder monkey"—a miner experienced in using explosives—wanted to set it up. Then he stuffed the dynamite into the holes, four or five sticks to a hole, and attached detonator caps and fuse as he moved around the hole pattern. The center holes were set to go off first and the others to follow, *boom, boom, boom,* always having a place to break to. Usually the lifters, the bottom row, detonated last to blow everything else into the middle for the mucking machines to scoop up and shove down the chute to be dropped into ore-skips.

When the round was ready to blow, the miners left the stope. The powderman carried the end of the fuse with him and used a spark to set off the detonator cords and the detonator cords set off the caps and the caps set off the dynamite. James showed me dynamite sticks—a silvery jell wrapped in white plastic. They were over an inch thick, a little over a foot long, and heavy. In the old days, the fuses were lit with matches.

"How are you doing?" James asked.

I'd forgotten to worry while he explained the dynamite process to me. "All right. I'm amazed at how much air there is. I'm not crazy about *this*," I admitted, looking up and feeling the mountain pressing in on me again, "but I'm not worried." I lied. "These lights are bright."

"It's frustrating for a miner to be outside at night with a flashlight, because it doesn't shine where you want it the way the headlamps do. If you talk to a miner on the outside, they always look at you like this." He turned his head slightly but still looked at me. "He never faces you so a light would shine in your eyes."

I realized my beam was shining in James's eyes, so I turned my head, too. I could still look at him, but my lamp pointed to the side.

"Do you want to go deeper?"

* * *

We went to another hoist station and waited. The man-skip was needed elsewhere for a while. The word *Quill* was painted on the rock wall in yellow paint. "What does that mean?"

"The Quill vein. Named after a miner who worked here maybe forty or fifty years. The veins are named after people: superintendents, shift bosses, miners who get killed."

"Does the vein go across or up and down?"

James shrugged. "Sometimes both. We traced Quill to below 15 Level and drilled for it on 17 Level but couldn't find it. It's bounded by rock strata north and south so the only thing we haven't determined now is top and bottom. We've got some good drill indications as high up as 5 Level, up in Wardner."

While we waited he talked about mining and miners. The miners wanted to get the rock out as much as the owners. They were paid, now, by the ton. But problems occurred. On any day there could be rock dropping or falling that needed extra time for barring down. Air pressure might be low so the mucker wouldn't run. He also explained about filling up sections of big stopes once they were partly mined to prevent cave-ins. The men built watertight fences across the drift into a stope and then slurry—a wet, sandy material left over from processing in the smelter—was piped into the played-out stope. At one section on 10 Level, we walked on grating across the top of a filled-in area. The slurry looked like quicksand.

"Everything looks corroded. Is that because of all the water?"

"Humidity. The water they bring in here has a lot of sulfuric acid, not enough to hurt anybody but it sure shows up." He pointed to the white cottony covering on the wall behind me. I'd noticed it earlier and wondered if lungs filled up with the same stuff.

"Why don't you teach anymore? Did the number of students drop when the mines closed?"

"This work pays better. Some families moved out, but a lot stayed, hoping the mines would open again." The man-skip slid silently to our floor and we climbed in. "Let's go to 23 Level. That's as deep as the mine is open now."

We had entered at Level 9, the level of the town, about 3,500 feet above sea level. I knew the mine levels had once gone to as low as 28 or 31. James dinged the bell.

Down we went, faster this time. As in an old-fashioned open elevator in a store, floors flashed past us. We slowed again for 23 Level, three hundred feet below sea level, so we were about two-thirds of a mile deep in the earth. We unloaded. The skip pulled up out of sight. By then, the temperature was quite warm, the humidity beginning to suffocate me. A faint fog seemed to swirl around, but I couldn't smell any rotten eggs. "James, I think I need to go back up."

"I could show you some more diggings down this way." He pointed to another black drift.

I bit my lip. Don't cry, I told myself. You're doing just fine. "Maybe not this time. Could we go up?" The weight of the mountain grew heavier and heavier on my brow.

James rang for the man-skip, which showed up almost immediately. By then, I was making myself take deep breaths, and gripping my hands into fists. I even welcomed the ride up and felt tons of earth move aside as we were pulled higher and higher by the cable.

At Level 9, I felt almost light-headed. We walked along the tunnel toward the main hoistroom.

"Do you need a toilet?" James asked.

"Do you read minds? Are there any?"

He stopped at a shack built against the wall and opened the door. To my relief, a real flush toilet sat there.

At Hoist no. 1, Virl greeted me. "Ready to go?"

His familiar face and steel-gray hair looked like an angel's. "Any time you are."

On the way out, I knew I wanted to learn more: how and why the miners did this work, why they spent their lives working underground and in the smelter and zinc plant for Bunker Hill. With men like Virl and James and the others, the town of Kellogg thrived from the late 1800s into the 1980s. Without the mine, I wondered if it would survive much longer.

The man-train chugged out of the Kellogg Tunnel about noon. Kissing the ground occurred to me, but I didn't want to embarrass Virl. I fingered the self-rescue kit, glad there had been no reason to open its lid.

11

Timberer, Miner, the Whole Shot

"I'm a miner, I'm a mucker, I'm a mean mother-trucker."

Epitaph at Greenwood Cemetery

During my youth, lights shone at the mill and rockhouse all day and all night. The mine whistle blew at every shift change. Once a day at least, the pent-up steam and gases in the blast furnace were released in a giant *whooosh*. Trains chugged on the tracks below the hospital parking lot, bringing in ore from other mines for processing, picking up products from the smelter and zinc plant—lead and zinc bars and concentrates or fines.

Smelter smoke never let us forget we lived in a mining town. Steam and sulfuric acid and some lead particles were pumped into our atmosphere all day and all night. Most days, a brown haze hung over the town. Some days, the prevailing westerly winds blew it up the valley. After I was exposed to clean air in Seattle and then returned for visits, my throat felt raw, my eyes watered, and my chest felt tight. While I was growing up, I hardly noticed the smoke. The same might be said for the mines themselves.

And until I went down into the mine in 1990, I did not appreciate what the miners and smeltermen, many of them my friends' fathers, did for a living. I spent half a day inside one, and I was afraid. College boys from Kellogg, and high school boys too, had worked around Bunker Hill every summer. Some men worked in the mines for a while and moved on to other jobs and professions, but many miners spent their lives working in the Bunker Hill or moving from mine to mine in the valley or the West. I wondered if they were afraid. Or if the dark and danger underground weighed them down. Did those working aboveground fear lead poisoning in the smelter or acid burns in the zinc plant? Only after I interviewed several of the miners did I realize why they stayed.

My picture of the mine was a sidecut of a rabbit warren with nesting areas and tunnels leading up and down from one area to another. A mine is much more complex, as I learned on my tour, but my image wasn't completely off. Missing from the rabbit warren were the sweat of men, the smell of sulfur, the haze of smoke from blasting, and the shrill keen of a drill.

Jim Bening's experience in the mines began in the mid-1930s and continued through the 1940s, although he began his career in Kellogg by following his father's footsteps, in logging. "I was loggin' but I didn't make enough money to keep the whole family goin' all winter. I had three kids, and to make ends meet, I worked underground all one year. Only took one day off—Christmas Day. At that time, I was makin' $4.50 a day. I was timberer, miner, the whole shot. The hardest work was sinkin' shafts, when you go from one level to the other, the vertical. There was no mechanical mucking machine, just that No. 2 shovel, and a bucket. It's a different world now because they have more technology. Makes the whole thing a hell of a lot easier."

This was a description of basic work in the mine: digging shafts from one level of the mine to another and then following the veins between levels by drilling, blasting, and mucking out. It was true in the '30s and it was true in the '80s.

"Before you had electrical headlamps," Jim said, "it was all carbide lamps. They were a lamp with a little bowl in it that you put maybe two or three ounces of carbide in. Then up above was a little container with a water control on it so you could give it more water. When it dripped on the carbide, you started it with a flint, and the flame would shoot out two or three inches. It was kind of dangerous. Goin' up them ladders, when you first went to work there, first thing you'd do is burn all the skin off the back of your hand."

* * *

Virl McCombs, the man who took me down the mine, came from South Dakota after the war to visit relatives. He signed on at the Bunker in 1946, and worked underground for thirty-four years. His primary job was hoistman, but he also worked as skip-tender, loading ore onto the skips to be brought back to the main level for transport out of the mine.

"Where I was working on the hoist, I never got to see the men. I sat back in an area by itself. The men would go down to different levels to their stopes and they'd mine them out. All I went by was the flash system. Flashing for a skip would be two bells and then one. That would be 9 Level. Then you start 2/1, 2/2, 2/3, and go on like that. Every level is a different signal."

The hoistman kept a logbook, noting any events during the day. Numbers for levels marked the big metal wheel like a clock. Level 9—the one we entered on—was at 1:00, Level 10 at 12:00, Level 14 about 9:00, and so on. He watched the circle as he let the skip down and, at the desired level, stopped the arrow at the mark on the wheel. In the hoist shack, the "flashes" for the skip sounded like knocking. On the lower levels, they dinged like bells.

"You can control the speed from 0 to 800 feet per minute, for men," Virl said. "On the other hoist, strictly for hauling ore, it would get up to 1,600 feet per minute. This was all controlled by the hoistman. One time I was in my hoist room and a guy came in and said, 'Boy, just think. Our life was in your hands the whole time we was in there.' A hoistman has a lot of responsibilities."

When Virl wasn't working hoist, he tended skip. The muckers moved the rock blasted out during the day shift to the chutes, with a shovel in the early days, as Jim Bening did, and later with the mechanical mucker. A chute held the ore until a skip-tender opened the door at the bottom and filled the ore cars one at a time until a full train was ready to transport its load to the ore-skips to be hoisted out of the mine. As a skip-tender, Virl opened those doors, filled the cars. If the ore jammed in the chute, the skip-tender had to loosen it by climbing up into the chute and barring down the clog or placing dynamite sticks—a dangerous job indeed. If he wasn't fast enough, the whole load could release and crush him.

"What keeps the stopes and drifts from caving in is the timber," Virl said. "It would be just like kids that build these little sets, square sets, cribbing." The mine consumed almost 7.5 million board feet of timber every year.

* * *

Dee Tatham, my friend Betty's father, was a hardrock miner for much of his working life. "I started mining when I was about eighteen. Starvation got me into it." He chuckled, but he meant what he said. Like Virl when I talked with him, Dee still worked hard, but not for other people any more. He tended his own small farm and garden, raising a calf or two, growing some alfalfa, building a shed, repairing tools, setting fence. At almost eighty, his hair was sparse and white, his face seamed, not unlike the Indian faces Edward Curtis photographed at the turn of the twentieth century.

The Tathams retired to a double-wide trailer home on acreage outside Sandpoint, Idaho. Over a huge farm dinner of fried chicken, mashed potatoes, gravy, green beans, salad, and apple pie for dessert, Dee told stories and drew diagrams of the kind of work he did. I didn't understand much of what he said until I traveled down into the mines myself.

Dee was only a wink away from a laugh as he told his stories. "One day I had to go in early, I and two other miners. They only had the ore-skip on. Earlier it had got away from them and left a pile of muck on the track. When we were going down in the man-skip, it hit that muck pile and kind of hesitated a little bit, and all that cable coming down pushed the skip over the pile. That skip was the same as being loose until it took all the slack out of the cable. We went down about one hundred feet, and we went back up like a yo-yo. We got thrown right down to the bottom of the skip. One guy said, 'Boy, when they take that skip out to overhaul it, they'll still be able to see my fingerprints.' "

Mining in Colorado, Dee said, was different from mining in the Bunker. "The way they did it in Colorado was you'd take off into a stope, from the top down. Fill in as you went along. Take out a whole stope, then leave the chute and manway timbered all the way down. Bunker Hill would go from the bottom up. It's safer to go from top down. And riding down the man-skip on an incline. Only the Bunker had that. The elevator is a whole lot safer. When you go down on an angle, you got the whole mountain above you. Straight down, it's on the side."

Later, I knew what he meant. I'd been keenly aware of the mountain, a scant twelve inches above my head when I rode the man-skip to 23 Level.

"Down there between 27, 28, and 29 levels—that was the richest silver that Bunker Hill had and it's still there. I used to run that little hoist down on 26½, called a 'sink hoist.' We had benches behind me where a lot of guys would come and eat lunch. I'd listen to all them shifters and bosses argue about how they're going to mine that ore out of there. They was afraid to go up underneath it, but that was the only way they knew how to mine it. It was so heavy with ore they was afraid they was going to get men killed. I coulda told them how to go and mine it safe, like in Colorado. But then, I was just a peon." The laugh wasn't in Dee's voice anymore.

After the trip into the mine on the man-train and the trip down to various levels on the man-skip, the shift miners arrived in the stopes. They took metal bars and "scaled" or "barred down" the ceiling or headwall, which means they scraped at the rock to see if anything else was going to fall. Once they were satisfied that the work area was relatively safe, the miners used the jackleg drill (jackleg is a name derived from Cornish miners, Cornish Jacks). Dee said, "You have controls and when you drill up high, you can move the leg up. Then you can drill another hole underneath the first one, and then release the air. You got to hold it. It's heavy. Or it will go jumpin'." Once he finished drilling holes, he wired each one.

Dee's specialty was blasting. "What you do is take a stick of powder—it's yellowish in color and wrapped in wax paper—and you got a powder knife and you slit it along the side and when you push it up, the powder bulges out. Take your load stick and tap it up the hole you've drilled." He gestured the tapping motion. "You slip the blasting cap on the fuse and clamp it. Put your primer on your fuse, same thing as a blasting cap. You're supposed to have clampers to clamp it on, like a little old pair of pliers. Everybody is supposed to use that, but mostly we clamped them with our teeth." Dee demonstrated, biting his teeth with bared gums. "It'd be dangerous if you bit too hard on one end of it." I imagined what the cap would do if it exploded in a man's mouth.

"You didn't want to get it on you or you'd get a headache. It had a lot of glycerin in it."

As he tamped the powder sticks into the drill hole, he loaded fuse with the blasting caps attached. "A lot of people tied the fuses together. That's what I did. You cut the fuses off. Cut the center ones off short and the outside, use longer ones, maybe two inches longer. You'd make a big round ball and they'd be sticking out there. Sometimes a fuse won't light right off and then you got to watch it. You had to have a fuse match, strike it on a rock, light the fuses, and get out of there. Anymore they're electrical. Next shift comes in, they muck it out."

* * *

Virl described the ventilation systems as fifteen different fans at ten separate locations circulating 150,000 cubic feet of air per minute. "When they blasted it would get pretty foggy, gas from the explosion more than anything else. From the day shift, they got out about 3:30, there'd be about a two-hour time period to clean the air out of the mine, let fresh air circulate before the next shift come in to the stopes to muck out. There wasn't all that much dust."

And air was not the only concern. Water seeped into the mines all day and night. Without constant pumping, the mine would have flooded. Almost two thousand gallons of water were pumped out of the 135 miles of underground tunnels and shafts every minute of every day, 365 days a year. Bunker Hill provided all the electricity and water used in Kellogg and Wallace from the beginning of the mine operations in the late 1800s until 1956, when the towns took over the operation of the utilities for their residents.

Virl talked about the processing of the ore, too. "Ore trains bring it out to the rock house. It was crushed there, then belted from there to the mill, going through another crushing system. They had steel balls, just like a cement mixer. The mixer would be turning and the balls would keep tumbling and crush this ore until real fine, and then it went by rail, the high line train, to the smelter. There it goes through a floating system in the smelter where it is melted in a molten process. Some waste went into the slag heap, all black because it was burnt. Other waste went to the mill ponds. It was kind of a sludge like affair."

* * *

Chuck Biotti began work as a mucker for Bunker Hill on March 7, 1930, and retired as a crane engineer on March 1, 1979. "I worked down in the mine for fifteen days. It didn't scare me going down the skip, but you know everybody says don't go in the stopes until a miner goes in and investigates, you see, because they blast the night before. Somethin' told me, you better stay out of there for a while. We worked about ten minutes and then just left. We moved back about fifty feet and down come a whole load. It took almost a day to clean up the mess. From then on, I didn't care much for that. I lost my appetite workin' in the mine. I couldn't eat, couldn't sleep.

"I was sixteen. I lied about my age, told 'em I was eighteen. I went to see Doc McCaffery. He says, 'Well, you get out of that mine and you'll be all right.' "

Chuck found a job on the track, where the receiving bins were unloaded. "They get all of the ore from the mines, coke and lime rock and all that stuff, that goes into the separate bins and then goes down into the mill and it's crushed and mixed and then it's carried to the smelter and roasted, you know, with phosphorus and so forth." Roasting removed the sulfur and created a product referred to as "sinter."

The sinter went to the blast furnaces where, under very high heat, 2,300 degrees Fahrenheit, it separated into two products: lead bullion and waste (slag), which floats on top of the bullion. Zinc was recovered from the slag by subsequent treatment. The bullion was further refined by the removal of copper, arsenic, and antimony. Another process recovered gold and silver. After the impurities were reduced in this process, the final product was cast into one-hundred-pound lead "pigs." Silver was also cast into bars. Both the pigs and bars were shipped elsewhere for use in final industrial or consumer products.

Chuck continued: "I worked in all the departments up at the smelter in the first two or three years. We was getting ore in boxcars and unloaded by hand. Four men to a car, two hours to a car to unload sixty tons of concentrates. We unloaded three cars a day with shovels. We got good exercise, built up our muscles."

At three dollars a day to start, Chuck earned top wages at the smelter. During the Depression, a supervisor called the men together at the lunch hour. At the time, lead was two cents a pound and zinc was a half-cent a pound. He gave the men a choice: lay off half or work the whole crew at half-time. "We told him we would rather work three days a week, so everybody went on three days and no one was laid off. Payday was on the 14th and 28th of every month. Our paycheck was eighteen dollars for two weeks and thirty-six dollars for a month. That thirty-six dollars was quite a bit because everything else went rock bottom.

"You could buy a loaf of bread for seven cents, eggs were eight cents a dozen, hamburger, six pounds for a quarter. This was in 1932, '33, and when I got married in 1935, I was getting eighty-five dollars a month. We rented a house at eighteen dollars a month from old man Papesh. Then you could buy a load of wood three dollars a cord for cooking on a wood stove. Three fryers for a dollar. A brand new Ford, that was $745. My wife and I used to go to shows for twenty cents. We could save just enough. Once a week, the Rena Theatre had 'pal' nights—two could go for the price of one.

"Things started getting better in 1934, started picking up a bit. In 1938, we had saved enough money to make a down payment on a 1938 Chevrolet—$950. We run that old Chevrolet—it wouldn't hold more than five gallons of gas. Sit in the back seat and your feet would look through the floorboard. In 1951, we traded it in and got $150. I was tickled to death. We bought another Chevrolet then for $1,800.

"In 1940, I went to operating a crane, loading things on the railroad cars. I operated one for thirty-five years. It was steam at first. Then they went to diesel-electric. We had ore coming in from Wallace, Mullan, Goldhunter, the Hecla, and the Broken Heel in Australia—lot of foreign ore."

In 1944, Chuck also joined the police force and he stayed on the auxiliary force for forty years. If he worked the day shift at the smelter, he worked swing as a policeman and vice versa. "If you want work," he said, "there is work to be done."

I asked him when he slept.

"After my swing shift—either on the high line or on the police—I come home at eleven, sleep from about midnight to six in the morning. Then at six, get up and have breakfast and drive out to the smelter, change clothes and I'm ready to go to work at seven. Weekends, if someone was sick on the department, or in the summer times, I worked every single day."

And what about vacations?

"Oh no. On *salary* you get vacation."

12

I Thought You Was a Goner

Dee Tatham faced one of his worst experiences at the Bunker Hill in the 1950s, where he worked as a powder man. No matter how careful a miner was, accidents still happened.

Dee balanced on a narrow ledge in the dark shaft and leaned his weight against the sweating rock wall of the raise. Sticks of powder —the dynamite—and primers weighed down the pockets of his work apron. Fuse line coiled from the clip around his waist. Out of the rock and earth, water dripped onto his hard hat, reminding him of snowmelt when he worked powder in Greenland.

The shaft he was raising, a space about four-by-eight feet, would extend from one drift level to the next, a distance of over a hundred feet. He'd already blasted around thirty feet, and below him, he and his partner, Pickles, had timbered up in two sections, half for the manway with the ladder down to the drift tunnel, his exit out, and half for the muck chute. The mixture of galena ore, mud, and rock was shoved down to where a tender would release it into ore cars to be trained out of the mine to the mill. He was, along with Pickles, assigned to blast the raise up through the rock. Then the miners would begin a crosscut, a horizontal drift along the vein.

Pickles drilled the inch-wide holes straight up with a jackleg drill, after he and Dee took turns barring down any loose rock, left over from the previous day's blow. It was just as Pickles said: "Can't trust them muckers on swing. How do we know they done a good job?"

One or the other of them nearly always mentioned Two-fingered Jack. Six months ago, the whole chute collapsed on him while he was packing powder. Accidents happen, but the men on shift changed over and again, so Dee and Pickles always double-checked. Newer miners didn't have the sixth sense, the feel for the ore; some of the older miners grew careless over time, or their luck ran out.

While Pickles sorted out the equipment and cables and moved tools and left-over timbers down the drift to clear the bottom of the chute, Dee prepared and loaded the powder. One by one, he inserted the dynamite into the holes above him and tamped them up with a wooden rod, seven or eight sticks to a hole. After the fourth or fifth stick, he stopped to measure and cut fuse, enough for six minutes burn time, and then he inserted the fuse end into a primer, filled with glycerin. With a wooden dowel, he pressed a hole into the end of a stick, crimped the primer on the fuse with his teeth, being careful not to bite too hard—he didn't want to blow his face off—and slotted the primer into the dynamite. Once the primed stick was in the hole, he pressed the next several tubes up as gently as he could with the tamping rod. The mine was dark and warm around him, damp and close. This day, outside, snow was blowing and drifting. The temperature had been fifteen below zero when he and Pickles had climbed into the man-train heading into the mine. A Greenland kind of day.

Blowing a raise was slow, arduous work. In a stope, the powder was set in a wall perpendicular to the floor. In the raise, Dee had to place the explosives above his head, so the blast dropped the muck straight down. A large piece of wood lagging protected the manway side of the shaft so the explosion would send the muck down the chute side. When each hole was loaded and fuses lit, Dee would climb down to a pigeonhole, a spot in the timbers between the muck chute and the manway, where he could re-enter the manway and step down the ladder into the tunnel below.

Each hole he plugged with Pilgrim Hats, small round pieces of metal. Only the fuses hung loose. He whistled between his teeth, a tuneless ditty that stopped whenever he had trouble with a plug. The shortest fuse hung from the center hole. It had to go first, so the rest could blow into the middle. He gathered the fuse ends and twisted all eight together.

"All clear?" Dee shouted down the hole.

"All clear." The answer floated up.

Dee struck a match and touched the end fuse. Sparks lit the shaft and outlined his slender shadow against the wall. He dropped down to a ledge opposite the entrance of the pigeonhole to safety. When he turned to shine his light on the fuses, checking to see they were all going, he mentally patted himself on the back for the way the fuses were looped and the fire slowly crept toward the Pilgrim Hats. Just then, the rock under his feet gave way. Before he could get any purchase on his escape hole, he dropped six feet into the chute. His hard hat jolted loose and fell, with the light, down and out of sight. He jammed his feet against the other side of the chute before panic froze him in place in the pitch dark.

All he had was six minutes. Less because he'd stopped to check. If he dropped, he'd break a leg or worse and the whole load would land on his head. Chill swept through him and almost made him lose his grip.

"Calm down, Dee old boy," he told himself. "Calm down."

He used up twenty seconds taking deep breaths. A scene flashed in his head. The day before, while Pickles drilled, Dee had pounded timbers into place to shore up the side of the chute and placed twenty-penny nails up one side as handholds while he worked. With one foot, he felt gingerly around for the top of the cribbing lining the chute. When he felt the uppermost timber, he balanced on one foot and scrooched his body down so he could feel around with his hand. Nothing. The soft ripping noise of the burning fuses sounded loud in his ears but their light didn't extend to him. He shifted his position because he could feel his foot slipping.

Another thirty seconds, maybe more, ticked by.

He inched himself up a foot or so by pressing his upper body against the timbered side of the chute and walking his feet up the lagging, worm-style. He could feel sweat pouring off his head, down his face. Fright tried to seize his mind, freeze him in place, but he took his right hand, found nothing, then his left, and felt along the corners of the timber. His finger struck a nail.

"God help me," he mumbled. His legs shook from the pressure or from fear. He found the second nail and knew he had the line. The nails weren't meant to hold a man, but if he moved fast enough, he thought they would. "Okay, Dee. Go!"

One boot, one nail. Second nail and then third. He clambered up on the nails, his hands trying to shift his weight. One nail slipped and he began to fall back and then his hand groped into emptiness— the pigeonhole. He pulled his body into it, felt across empty space for the metal ladder in the manway. The pitch of the burning fuses became a roar in his head. Flesh met steel.

In four rapid skips, like rappelling down a mountain, Dee jumped to the drift floor at the bottom of the chute. To his left, he could see a faint glow, probably Pickles's light. He ran in stumbling jerks through the squashy mud and water toward it. Dull whumps and the smell and fog of sulphur followed him, knocking him to his knees. Pickles ran toward him, grabbed him, and pulled him against the wall.

"Where the hell you been? I thought you was a goner."

"Me, too, Pickles." Dee closed his eyes and caught his breath. He sagged in his partner's arms. "Oh, Christ, me too."

* * *

Dolly Parker's husband, Gordie, wasn't quite so lucky. "Gordie had his accident after we moved to Wardner. He was head timberman. There was a big rock hanging down that looked bad. He told the men, 'You better get out from under that rock and get the tools out.'

"And the fellow down there said, 'Which rock?' He poked at it, and it came down on Gordie's back. He was in a wheelchair for thirty-two years. Brought him out on a stretcher. Strapped him down and took him up the hoist."

*   *   *

Lead poisoning was a threat to the workers from the beginning of the operation of the smelter. In one publication, I saw a photo of men with their arms and legs in tubs of water through which a small electric current was passed. This treatment, used in 1921, was supposed to remove lead from the body. Periodic urinalysis testing helped find miners with elevated lead conditions. When my father doctored in Kellogg, the workers with lead were treated mostly by removing them from the bag house and smelter and reassigning them to other locations around Bunker.

The men I talked to who had worked in the mines and the smelter made their jobs seem like ordinary work, something the men went to every morning and for which they collected their pay every week. Charles Rinaldi referred to the work as "easy" for his father, after the stone masonry work in Italy.

In fact, the mining jobs were difficult and dangerous. They didn't sound or look easy at all. The strength mining required, the dirt and darkness, the heat and sense of the mountain pressing down, and most of all, the ever-present danger of rock bursts, crippling accidents, and fire—these working conditions appalled me. Although my descent was in 1990, mining methods had changed only slightly since the late 1800s to take advantage of new technology, such as electricity, pneumatic and then hydraulic drills, new generators, the pumping of slurry back into the mines to fill mined-out stopes, and new and more efficient refining techniques. Over the years, the number of men needed underground decreased, but the men who remained still performed the same jobs.

The teacher who was my guide inside the mine also took me through the smelter, but this was during a period when little smelting of minerals was occurring because the output from the mines had diminished considerably and the Environmental Protection Agency had closed down many aspects of the operation. My guide was a member of the mine safety team. I asked him what one should do in case of fire. This was his advice:

"If you can't get out, sit down near an air hose. Wrap a raincoat over you. Before that, stack up boards if you can find any, giving yourself some space, and build a seal. This will keep smoke and fire from coming to you, and keep the air from fueling the fire."

* * *

Virl and a fellow hoistman, Lee Seufert, met with me in the fall of 1998. Lee began work in the Bunker in 1940, left to serve during World War II, and returned to work steadily from 1945 to 1981. His beginning pay was $4.95 a day and on the last day he was earning $12.50 an hour. He worked the no. 3 hoist that operated from 23 Level down to 29 Level for twenty-seven years. The "gyppo" miners, independent contractors who were paid by the ton of ore mined, could earn over $40,000 a year by the time the mine closed, compared to $25,000 or so for the hourly miner.

"There was always a lot of tramp miners. You know that flagpole out by the dry house? When the sunshine hit the tip of the pole, they'd leave. And I mean right that minute! Climb out of the man-cars and take off—heading to the woods to go huntin', or just movin' on."

They swapped some hoistman stories and Virl said, "After a while you got to know the skip-tenders by the way they flashed." Lee talked about working double shifts to make extra money or to cover for someone.

"Mining was a good job," he said. "It paid good money. Miners are a different breed. They're easy-goin', jokin'. There never were fights inside. I knew so many great guys. If they couldn't read or write, or couldn't even speak English, it didn't matter. Any kid in high school could get a job in the summer, and I mean boy or girl. In the zinc plant, sweepin', office. Everybody at Bunker was treated pretty darn good."

* * *

Miners' pay ratcheted up over the years, from per day to per hour to per ton. Women joined the men in the drifts and tunnels and crosscuts. Health risks decreased and safety measures improved. But up until the Bunker closed in 1981, mining remained hard work. The threat of danger below ground every hour and every day perhaps sparked the wilder life on the surface. The high wages attracted workers, kept them there. Community life, hunting and fishing, and even the constant temperature underground figured in the equation, too. The work ethic passed from grandfather to father to son: Drill, blast, muck out. Rock in the box. Crush it. Smelt it. Ship it out.

13

He'd Have to Pay Me like a Man

While the men who came to Kellogg went to work for the Bunker, and their sons followed in their footsteps, the wives and daughters often went to work, too.

Betty's mother, Dora, worked at Pat's Boarding House for twenty-four years. Dora's stories were familiar to me because Betty and I used to change beds at the Pleasant Home, a rooming house run by her parents, on a Saturday morning. In sun-filled rooms, we tore off sheets, snapped open clean ones, and whipped them on aging mattresses. Man smells—tobacco, sweaty socks and undershirts, and mint after-shave lotion—lingered.

"When I first went to Pat's," Dora said, "we had about 210, 230 men, all day. It was three dollars a day for board and room. They were just little rooms, big enough, some of them had two beds. The men packed their own lunches and also packed lunches for half the workers in the mine.

"At Pat's we cooked breakfast, and then we had lunch. And then we had an evening meal. I worked fourteen, sixteen hours a day. When I first started, I made breakfast and then I'd make the beds. After the full-time cook quit, I got breakfast and came back in the afternoon for the evening shift. I had to be there at 4:00 A.M. for breakfast. We put the lunch stuff out on a long table and the miners made lunches while we cooked breakfast. I'd get about two hundred

101

breakfasts in the morning, serving just about everything—bacon, eggs, sausage and ham, French toast, hotcakes, hash browns.

"At the evening meal, it was all the same menu—steak, hamburgers, stew, roast beef, roast pork. It wasn't short orders. I did all the ordering from 1959 on. For a while we got the food down by the railroad track, that big warehouse. Most of the stuff came from Spokane. The meat we got from Brewers up in Wallace at Nine Mile. I ordered once a week. We bought our meat and stuff, by the half or whole beef. One of the Rinaldi brothers used to come and cut up the meat for us.

"We'd start serving at 5:00 in the morning. They'd come to the window and order. We cooked bacon and sausage and had it all ready. All we had to do was cook eggs. Two or three women helped out on the floor. I worked split shift when I first started. I done everything—washed dishes, cooked, made the beds."

Dora and Dee bought the boarding house in the early 1960s and Dora ran it by herself. "I had it until 1974. The way they set up was, the Bunker allowed me so much. If I didn't make it, they reimbursed me. They paid the bills. There was a lot of times when I made more than the bills. I got to keep whatever it was.

"We finally dwindled down from some two hundred boarders to about thirty when I closed it. We got so we couldn't even furnish bedding. They'd come out of the mine and just crawl into bed. It was terrible. Drugs, marijuana and stuff was starting. We started going downhill from there. After the slot machines went out, that was when just drifters came, and it wasn't lively like it was. We didn't gamble. No slots in the boarding house. But the miners did gambling every night, every night they had a dollar. That little town was wild."

Some women also worked in the mine or in mining operations. Jim Bening, who was single during the 1940s and most of the '50s, knew a fair number. "It was after the war they mostly came in," he said. "They worked in the labs and they done a lot of clean up. They worked in the zinc plant and in the smelter. They had someone takin' care of the lights in the mine. Bunker had 150 to 200 women there. They were very nice, hard working, trying to keep their families together. Most of the time they didn't have a husband, you know. Had nice kids. Good pay."

Virl's friend Lee remarked on women working as miners. "In the '70s, women started working in the mines. I remember Little Heavy —she probably weighed one hundred pounds soaking wet. Foreman put her on as a skip-tender. I told him she can't do it and I'd say the same for a little man. So he gave her some men to help out. She got hurt—crushed her fingers, and she drove herself all the way to Spokane, crushed hand and all, and got 'em sewed up."

*　*　*

Hazel Corbeill came to Idaho from Canada with her parents, who operated a cafe in Mullan and then in Kellogg. She worked at the cafe from the time she was very young, standing on a stool over the sink to wash dishes, cut vegetables into soup crocks, readied lunches for miners. When allowed, she attended school and loved every subject she studied. After she won a prize for an essay she wrote, her parents forced her to marry at the age of sixteen because she was "getting above herself." The man she married, she said, was a miner who spent most of his paycheck in the bars rather than bringing it home so Hazel could clothe their two boys and put food on the table. Finally, she went to work herself, clerking at a dry goods store, learning how to handle money, make deposits, order stock. She divorced her husband at a time when divorces were almost unheard of, and managed to take care of herself and her two boys. From the dry goods store, she moved to a flower store and was so successful, she bought the store herself.

Kellogg Flowers was a store on Main Street. Hazel arranged for flower delivery, brought in fresh flowers from Spokane and Missoula, and was one of the first women to operate a business in town. She joined a floral trade association and was actively sought after as a speaker on "how to do it," even though she was the only woman member. I could imagine this woman with her wild bushy hair, strong arms and shoulders, and firm opinions, standing in front of a group and indeed telling them how, why, when, and where to do their business.

When I talked with Hazel, she had long since retired, and lived in one of the Sunnyside houses by herself. Her second husband had died a number of years before after a long illness. Her shock of white hair was still her trademark, and although she seemed to have trouble getting around easily, she was still using her mind and heart to write about the early days in Kellogg. Her manner was often gruff, but she was full of gossip and stories, most of which she didn't want repeated. Sometimes, she seemed embarrassed by her humble beginnings and, other times, angry with her parents and certainly angry with the husband who was forced upon her. But she also knew she had accomplished more than many people with her successful business.

* * *

Dolly Parker went to work to support herself and her disabled husband, Gordie. During World War II, she worked as a police dispatcher. "I got my chance," she said, "to work at a job that paid good money. Not as much as a man, mind you. I was just a woman." When the war ended, she lost the job. Before long, though, the police chief called and asked her to come back as night dispatcher. "I said I'd come, but he'd have to pay me like a man. He hemmed and hawed and finally said okay. It's a good thing, too, because Gordie's back needed one operation after another."

Did you ever get tired, I asked, thinking of long nights at the station and long days nursing a sick husband.

"All the exciting things happened at night, like the time one of the prostitutes bit off a customer's ear, or police raided the gambling den at the Legion Hall. I liked working nights. I was gone while Gordie slept and pretty much the whole day I could keep him company. I never did sleep much. There were lots of hard times. The saddest ones, though, were when the kids got hurt or killed. Most often I was the one who had to call their folks. I recollect that pretty little blonde girl from down the way, when they found her in a car in the river."

I remembered too. The pretty blonde girl was a classmate of mine and hers was the first funeral I ever attended. The casket was open and her skin was pale as alabaster, except for her cheeks. They shone red with rouge, making her look like a made-up doll.

"I think the hardest year of my life was the year of the mine strike," she said. "It went on and on. I got laid off and we had no money, except Gordie's puny disability check. I did laundry and ironing again, but it was hardly enough to eat on. Then Gordie got sick. I tried to keep him at home because we couldn't pay the hospital bills, but your dad said he had to have the round-the-clock care. Gordie went downhill so fast. After he died, Doc sat up with me and him all night long. We talked about the old days and about Gordie on the fiddle and your dad on the drums. Somehow, sitting and talking eased my heart. Gordie had been happy and Doc helped me remember that.

"Those good times are pretty much all gone now. When the mines closed down, most folks just left. I hear they dug up the football field and spread new dirt around. I guess it's right, though. Plenty of poison got pumped out of that mountain. Plenty of jobs, too. I hear tell the trees are growing back up the mountainsides, just like when we first set up housekeeping. I'd sure like to know if there's live ones up Deadwood. Wasn't then and I bet there isn't now. Still, if I knew, I could tell Gordie when I see him."

*   *   *

Jessie Rinaldi went to Normal School in Lewiston to be trained as a teacher. In high school, she had worked at the local five-and-dime.

When she returned to Kellogg, she taught school in Wardner and lived with her parents. As she walked from Sunnyside up Depot Hill all the way to Wardner, she sometimes passed a young man who would smile at her on his way to work in the mines. One evening, she stayed for dinner at a boarding house near where she taught and there met LaVern, the smiling miner. Before long, they married and moved to Los Angeles, where he went to electricians' school. By the time they returned to Kellogg, the Depression had begun and the only work LaVern could find was again in the Bunker Hill Mine.

"I wanted to work," Jessie said, "but you see they wouldn't hire married teachers. We could substitute, and they asked me to take the second grade up there at Washington for six months. So I taught then.

"In the Depression, it was pretty rough, but we had fun. I tell you, it was good for people, because then you really appreciate when you do get higher up and money that you don't have to worry about. It was just wonderful. I think it was good for us, but I would hate to see our children go through it because they are so used to having everything. I don't think they could take it. We were always kind of poor, although Dad did very well."

My friend Judy's mother, who also grew up in Kellogg, had been a teacher, too. When she married Judy's father, they kept their marriage secret for a year until he could get established as a young lawyer in town. Once their secret was out, she ceased teaching and was active in all the ladies' clubs and projects with my mother.

* * *

Nurses, all women then and mostly married, were the backbone of the Wardner Hospital. We children ran in and out and through the hospital and clinic and came in constant contact with pink-cheeked Mickey and Millie, the operating room nurses, red-haired Holly and Katie and Alice, and Janet, my father's nurse for seventeen years at the clinic and obstetrics nurse at the hospital. Always dressed in their crisp white uniforms, hose, shoes, and usually white starched winged caps, they fulfilled my visions then of angels in the Florence Nightingale mode. Janet's first job out of nursing school at the hospital paid $335 a month in the 1950s. "When a doctor walked into the room," she said, "we stood." My father saw so many patients every day, I knew he relied heavily on the nurses' able assistance. He couldn't have done it without them.

"There was good nursing and good doctoring at Wardner Hospital," Janet said. "Some of the cases there wouldn't have had a ghost of a chance anywhere else."

*   *   *

Although my mother drew road maps for a living while my father was in medical school, in Kellogg she did the kind of work more usual for women in the era in which she grew up. In addition to painting, she volunteered: editing her Alpha Chi Omega sorority newsletter and working for the University of Idaho Alumni Association or Foundation, meeting with the state and local medical auxiliaries and participating in the American Medical Association's political action group (as a Republican), and attending meetings of her numerous women's clubs—PEO, Eastern Star, AAUW, Study Club.

Almost fifty women in town belonged to the American Association of University Women. They were teachers and the educated wives of mine personnel and business and professional men. They represented schools from all over the West, often the same schools where their husbands earned degrees in engineering and mining studies. Others came from the East: Carnegie, Chicago, Queens, and Mt. Holyoke, to name a few. Mother said their interests in AAUW were education, the status of women, the importance of the educated woman in determining the quality of life in the community, and national issues. Each year, they presented a Senior Tea for the girls at Kellogg High School. The tea table was "beautiful with silver service, petit fours, cookies, and the fanciest of finger sandwiches," according to my mother. The deans of women from the local universities spoke to the girls, as the primary purpose of the tea was to encourage all seniors to go to college. The AAUW also held workshops on money management for the townswomen.

Another organization my mother served was the Shoshone County Medical Auxiliary—doctors' wives in the county. They planned their activities at monthly luncheons and raised money through rummage sales, book reviews, bridge luncheons, tea tastings, and an annual dinner dance. All funds went for scholarships for nursing students, beginning in 1949 with $75, and continuing into the 1990s with $1,100 for any health-related field. In recent times, they sponsored AIDS films in the schools, awareness campaigns for infant seats and use of seat belts, and health topics for teens and the aged.

The Kellogg Study Club began in 1919. I thought of it when I read *And Ladies of the Club* by Helen Hooven Santmyer because membership was by invitation only and was limited to twenty women. My mother joined in 1950. Their main money raiser was the Harvest Ball in November. Money from the dance went to buy eyeglasses for school children and sometimes to pay for operations. This club also met monthly—three misses and a member would be uninvited.

My mother's work and her organizations were as close to feminist groups as was possible in the 1950s. These women never thought of themselves that way—it wasn't in their vocabulary. But without their work, many girls would not have gone to college; many more students would have struggled with handicaps and poverty.

*   *   *

I didn't learn the term *in loco parentis* until I went to college, but in Kellogg, nearly everyone acted the part of a parent when we were growing up. A policeman stopped me one night on the road outside the drive-in just west of town. He recognized me as Dr. Whitesel's daughter, told me to slow down and if he stopped me again, he'd tell my dad. A girlfriend and her boyfriend tried to buy beer at a small tavern in Pinehurst. One of the customers said, "Aren't you in my daughter's class at school?" The two underage would-be beer buyers slinked out, beer-less.

No one locked the doors. When we visited back and forth, people simply walked in, calling "Yoo-hoo. Anybody home?" My friends stopped at our house for milk and cookies nearly every day after school. Most of us went home for lunch until we attended junior high and high school at locations too far to walk home. And then we ate in the cafeterias or lunchrooms together.

There was little separation between adults and children. We all lived our lives knowing each other, and, in our town, the young people were often on a first-name basis with most of the adults, not as a sign of disrespect, but as a sign of friendship. All the adults I knew said, "Call me Charlie," or Delia, or Elaine, or Scottie, or LaVernon, or George, Bob, or Bill. We learned the titles, of course—Dr., Mr., Mrs., Miss—but used them only in the workplace—school, hospital, office.

These people called each other by first names, too, again reflecting the informality and friendliness of the mining community. If they didn't interact at work, then they talked with each other at church or school or club meetings or on the street outside the drugstore, or while shopping at Hutton's Department Store or sitting in the stands at football and basketball games.

The miners, the doctors, the cooks and waitresses, the police, the night dispatcher, the service people, the small businesspeople like the florists and butchers and many more, the women's clubs, the bankers, the teachers—all of these people made up the communal mix of Kellogg.

So did a few others, who were rarely mentioned.

Winter view of Kellogg, Idaho, showing Bunker Hill lead smelter with the zinc plant in the background. Courtesy of Kellogg Public Library, Album F-26.

WARNING
HAZARDOUS MATERIALS
SUPERFUND SITE
NO TRESPASSING

Bunker Hill slag pile with the smelter in the background and fence circling all the works, ca. 1996. Photograph by Gerry Morrison.

Demolition scrap pile at Bunker Hill, inside fence enclosing all the works. Photograph by Gerry Morrison.

Marie and Glen Whitesel, parents of author, in Moscow, Idaho, ca. 1938. Photograph from the collection of Marie Whitesel.

Doc Whitesel in surgical clothes at Doctor's Clinic in Kellogg, 1964. Photograph from the collection of Marie Whitesel.

Wardner Hospital, located on McKinley Avenue in Kellogg, Idaho,
ca. 1947. Courtesy of Kellogg Public Library, Kellogg, Idaho.

Bunker Hill Mine entrance, 1990. Photograph by Gerry Morrison.

Julie Whitesel Weston on Level 23 during her 1990 tour of Bunker Hill Mine. Photograph from the collection of Julie Weston.

Down the shaft of Bunker Hill Mine, 1990. Photograph from the collection of Julie Weston.

Oasis Bordello Museum

605 Cedar Street
Historic Wallace, Idaho 83873
(208) 753-0801
(208) 752-3721

Menu

January, 1988

	Price	Minutes
Straight, no frills	$15.00	8
Straight, regular	$20.00	13
Half & Half, no frills	$20.00	11
Half & Half, deluxe	$25.00	15
Straight, French, no frills	$25.00	10
Straight, French	$30.00	15
"69"	$30.00	15
Half Hour	$35.00	
Per Hour	$70.00	
Bubble Bath & Half Hour	$50.00	
Bubble Bath & Hour	$80.00	

Positions, $5.00 ea. plus $2.00 ea.

Vibrator - $15.00 plus regular party price plus $5.00

Doubles - double price per party, time same as one

Oasis Bordello Museum menu, Wallace, Idaho. Courtesy of Michele Mayfield.

Lodge at Lookout Pass Ski Area, Idaho-Montana border, 1950s.
Courtesy of Kellogg Public Library, Album F-56.

Kellogg Senior High School on a foggy day in 2008. Photograph by Gerry Morrison.

Sunshine Miners' Memorial to the men who lost their lives in the Sunshine Mine disaster in 1972. Sculpture by Ken Lonn; photograph by Gerry Morrison.

Smelter stack blows in Kellogg, Idaho, in 1996. Photograph by Virl
McCombs.

14

Straight, No Frills— $15 for 8 Minutes

Both Kellogg and Wallace were known around the Northwest for their vices and, in particular, for prostitution. The most famous prostitute was Molly B'Dam, long since buried in the Murray cemetery. She came to the mining camps in the late 1800s, and her story borders on a common fable of western prostitutes: She was forced into prostitution but tended stricken miners during a cholera epidemic and gave her gold to those in need. Her own end came from tuberculosis.

Less romance surrounded the real story of prostitution, as gritty as Molly's was. Many prostitutes took drugs: opium and morphine. Most died young, from drug overdoses, from venereal disease, from abuse and gunshot wounds by pimps, from suicide and childbirth. Those who didn't die young aged early, sliding from the brothels on a circuit with steady customers, to flophouses, then to cribs and street-walking, and finally to disease and death, old and alone. A few stories were happier: prostitutes married their customers and became respected members of the community. Others made enough money and left the profession and the mining towns to lead productive lives elsewhere.

Which tales were true is sometimes difficult to tell. But one aspect of prostitution remained constant while I was growing up and for years before and afterward: it was always present. In Kellogg, the houses lined up along Railroad Avenue. In Wallace, the houses occupied brick buildings a block or two off the main thoroughfare through town, designated with the term "Rooms," and entered via stairways from the street.

Going to one of the houses was a rite of passage for teenage boys when I was in high school. "He's been to Wallace" were code words that the boy had done the deed, had become a man. We girls gossiped about it and acted as if we understood the ramifications. I'm not certain I did. The words "whore" and "cathouse" in those days were not spoken aloud in polite company, or even not-so-polite. "Houses" were commonly understood to refer to the brothels.

I met one of the prostitutes at the Robson Law Office, where I worked after school. Ginger was a big-boned woman, with a plain, flat face and reddish over-permanented hair. When she entered the office, she asked for my boss in a phlegmy, smoke-filled voice. Her clothes were nondescript, her shoes large. Nothing about her suggested her profession, nor did I know it until my boss told me. The probate of a will she brought in was that of a local madam, probably the last one before the houses were closed down by one mayor (who promptly lost the next election) and then demolished and covered over by the new freeway cleaving the town in half, right down Railroad Avenue. Perhaps the madam was Dixie.

Everyone has stories about prostitutes. Butch Brewer who owned a meat company up Nine Mile out of Wallace described the way these women were accepted in the Panhandle communities. "We had prostitutes up there. Big Edith. She was everybody's friend in town, just a neighbor. The only one I knew was Mickey. She was like your friend's sister. Everybody knew her. People accepted her. She was a large, blonde, pleasant-looking woman in her twenties. She had some rooms over the garage. She'd come in the meat market and store off and on. She was part of the community. I can't remember anyone making a complaint about her. You wouldn't call her sexy or anything, just kind of a wholesome girl next door."

Hazel told a story about prostitutes, too. "One of the biggies in town, the first time he came in to order some flowers, he wanted two dozen red roses, and he wanted us to deliver them to one of those houses. He had a nice big expensive car. Didn't want us to arrange a basket or anything. Then he paid for them, in cash, and they went to Dixie's I guess it was, the one by the railroad tracks, the one with the outside stairway. One of the girls there was celebrating her birthday. That man had half a dozen children and he and his wife lived in a nice place."

My employer, Bob Robson, loved to tell stories, and the following one indicated the exploitation of the prostitutes.

After the war, Bob worked at The Lighthouse, the local electric company, reading meters. He served half the town and someone else the other half. Each covered a whorehouse. One noon, the other meter reader said, "You gettin' any?"

"What are you talking about?" Bob asked.

"You got a whorehouse over there?"

"That old biddy scares me to death," Bob said. "She looks like if you touched her you'd get venereal disease."

"She's just the madam," the other meter reader said. "Don't pay any attention to her. She's got some good-looking girls in there. I'm getting free nooky." He had the Bridge Beer Parlor. "I go in and read the meter and double the reading. I knock on the door and ask if there is any reason why their electric bill ought to be so high this month. They always say no. I tell them it is going to be terrible high and do they want to take it out in trade. I say I'll take half of it out in trade and then they pay their regular bill."

Bob was floored. To me, he said, cackling, "That man was a dog-robber, but I always thought it was funny."

* * *

A tale that reflected the lives of the prostitutes came from one of my father's friends I'll call Will. "A couple of guys and I went to the whorehouse and took it over for the night. We locked the door and said we were going to be entertained and take care of everyone, see? Well, it got to be around two in the morning, this little girl about eighteen come in. I was taking a nap in one of them hooker's rooms.

"I heard them say you were a logger," she said. "My daddy's a logger."

"Yeah," Will said.

"I got in here and they're expectin' me to perform different sexual things that I refuse to take part in and they're slappin' me around quite a bit."

"If you want to get out of here, you come with me," Will told her. "We're going to leave pretty quick."

"I don't have any money."

His friend Hank came in about that time and Will said, "Give me twenty dollars, Hank." And he gave Will twenty dollars, and Will added twenty dollars and gave her the forty dollars. "So we got all ready to leave and we got pilin' out the door from upstairs. After the last one out, why, the door slammed and that little girl didn't make it. We could hear her screaming in there. The rest of them were just beating the hell out of her." Will and his friends arrived at Will's apartment, and he said, "We better call somebody."

Will called the police chief and said, "You better go over there. They're beating up on that little whore, and I don't think it's right."

"Oh, you goddam bunch of drunks. What are you gettin' me out of bed for?"

So Will called the FBI down in Coeur d'Alene. Nothing happened for a year. One night, Will was entering his apartment in Smelterville and the U.S. marshal waited for him. Will said, "I don't remember a damn thing about that." All the time the FBI was getting a case together, a white slavery case against the madam. Some pimps from Portland were involved.

In the end, Will was subpoenaed to testify in federal district court, partly, he said, because he was the only single man in the

bunch who called the FBI. "They got me up on the witness stand—
one of those stands you climb up about five steps and everybody in
the courtroom is looking at you. The little girl testified I had nothing to do with her except I give her forty dollars. I had no reason, just
because she told me her dad was a logger. This little hooker got
married and had a nice family. Her husband was sittin' there. She
had a very high regard for me. She said, 'That guy never even fucked
me or anything. I don't know why he gave me the money. Just to get
me away from there.' So the end result was that those pimps were
sent to the penitentiary and that landlady got five years."

Will had good words for the most famous living madam in the
county, Delores. "I was a personal friend of hers. A fabulous woman.
She always furnished the band uniforms for the high school and
uniforms for the police department, the whole shot. She had a hell
of a talent for taking care of everybody. She always got new hookers.
The pimps and whores had a route, a three-way deal from Winne-
mucca to Portland to Wallace. They kept rotating. Kellogg was never
one-tenth of what Wallace was when it came to hookers. Most of
them were eighteen years old."

Delores became almost as famous as Molly B'Dam. A Wallace
doctor said: "She was one of the nicest people I've ever met. She
didn't smoke or drink. She just simply said that miners are going to
do this thing and we want to help them be happy. She was a great
person to give money to charitable causes. Never did it in her
own name."

Everyone described Delores as beautiful. The closest I could get
to a description, though, was that she had black hair and finally
"got fat," according to the doctor's wife. The doctor tempered that
with "on the chubby side."

And Will told another story: "The miners would carry out drill
bits in their lunch buckets, you know, worth around five or seven
dollars apiece. Them hookers got on to it and you could get a piece
of tail there for one of those knockoff bits. Then the hookers would

sell them back to the Bunker. 'Course it was a different world then. The cost at the houses was only three dollars."

And another: "I know that some of the kids there in Kellogg all had the clap and didn't have any money for gas. They'd get up a carful and go see old Doc Stone up in Wallace. At that time they didn't have sulfa or penicillin. They used to irrigate it [the penis] with that potassium permanganate, that purple stuff. Quite a deal. A friend of mine worked on the railroad and he had clap for a long time. Someone told him if he raised his temperature up to 105, it would cure his disease. So he got a big washtub full of water there by the bridge at the mouth of the river near Enaville, and packed it up with branches from the apple trees in an orchard there. He stacked them all up and lit a fire under it. He stood the heat for so long, he just parboiled his ass. Still had the clap when he got through."

Even after slot machines and wholesale gambling disappeared, brothels stayed. The menu for services in one of the north Idaho brothels in January, 1988, was:

Straight, no frills	$15	8 minutes
Straight, regular	$20	13 minutes
Half & Half, deluxe	$25	15 minutes
Straight, French	$30	15 minutes
"69"	$30	15 minutes
Per Hour	$70	
Bubble Bath & Half Hour	$50	

A raid by the FBI on gambling in the taverns and bars a few years later scared the last "working girls" away. The Oasis Bordello Museum in Wallace, Idaho, offers a realistic look at their lives in the old Lux Rooms. For a small charge, it is possible to tour the upstairs rooms, where mannequins are dressed in negligees or bikinis, lipstick still sits on a dressing table along with spilled powder, all left on the day of the raid when the "girls" left town in a hurry. Fuzzy rugs with a path tramped through them cover the floors. The beds are narrow cots, the rooms small as cells. A series of wood boxes with slots for payment sit on top of the refrigerator in the kitchen, along with a number of alarm clocks. After each customer entered a room, the clock was set for fifteen or twenty minutes, depending on the payment. When time ran out, a runner went to the room and knocked on the door. Time's up!

The most famous reputed patron of Delores was one of the mine owners, who went on two- and three-week drinking binges, spending part or all of that time in her rooms. The Wallace doctor reported this story:

"I had a patient who needed to see [the mine owner] on business. I found out that he was at Delores's place and lucid enough to talk to my patient. He went down there and was showed into this room. There was Mine Owner sitting in the middle of this bed. There was a gal on every corner—four women. He was perfectly normal and sober and answered all the questions. And all the girls were naked."

15

How's Your Body? II

Upstairs at the hospital, wards held six to eight beds at a time: iron single beds, white linens, smooth floors, nurses in white shoes, casts held in the air with pulleys, men on crutches, pale from the neck down and dressed in blue robes. Because children were not generally allowed in the rooms, I was a rare visitor to the second and third floors. Only once did I go as a patient—a first-grader with pneumonia—and spent several nights, more incensed at having to sleep in a crib than I was sick. One of my father's partners extracted my brother's tonsils and we visited. The ice cream and milkshakes served to him seemed more than just recompense for the pain. I wanted my tonsils out, too, but no one listened.

The laundry room was in the basement, filled with the burnt-cotton odor of clothes tumbling in giant industrial dryers and the soapy smell of wash water. The floor and walls were concrete, like our own basement. My brother and I sneaked down, looking for a morgue, but we were afraid to open closed doors with cloudy glass windows. He scared me with tales of dead bodies waking and walking in the halls, of mummies groaning and finding us in our beds.

Death was not a subject we discussed around our house, although names of dread diseases often comprised the spelling quizzes my father gave at dinner time. Arteriosclerosis. Melanoma. Streptococcus. Pulmonary edema. Pneumonia. Poliomyelitis. Tuberculosis. I spelled most of them correctly, pandering to my father for approval, wishing to avoid forever the opprobrium he heaped on my brother—names like "stupid" and "nitwit" and sometimes a thump on the head.

Car wrecks were frequent occurrences in our valley. My father told gruesome stories of broken bones, disfiguring gashes, and swollen hematomas to serve as object lessons when my brother began to drive. No epidemics of disease hit our town, although a polio scare worried adults and kids alike. The doctors and nurses dispensed the first Salk vaccines at the schools and within weeks, two children contracted polio. The vaccine was blamed because it contained the live virus. My father said afterward that if we survived the shot, we'd never get the disease itself.

Stories filtered to us from friends' parents and other adults about my father's medical and diagnostic capabilities and his concern for his patients. He dropped everything to respond to a person in need, leaving the house in the middle of the night, driving out to the sticks to treat someone, staying with a patient all day and all night if need be.

One New Year's Day, my father stopped by the hospital to see his patient Nick, who was in a coma as a result of a stroke. Nick owned several bars in town, which his wife, Mary, struggled to keep going. She and their young son sat by Nick's side, talking, hoping he would wake up. Dad studied Nick, took his vital signs, then said, "I'll be right back." He went to the kitchen and returned with a short mason jar half-filled with whiskey. With one hand behind Nick's back, he lifted him and held the jar to his lips, slipping some of the liquid into his mouth. While they all watched, Nick licked his lips. That was the first movement he'd made on his own for weeks. Within a few more days, he was alert and sitting up. Before too long, he was at home and running his businesses again with the help of his wife. My father stopped by every week or so to check on him. His son said my father gave his father nine more years of life.

Bob Robson, the attorney I worked for in high school, was sick for a whole winter after leaving Guam, where he served as prosecuting attorney. In March he went to Dad for some oral penicillin. Back at his own office, Bob noticed a bump on his wrist and skin splotches. He returned to the hospital. My father gave him adrenalin, made him lie down, and watched him for a while before sending him home. There Bob's throat began to close. His wife Penny panicked. Bob told what happened next:

"It was after 5:00, and you were getting a driving lesson from your dad over on the airport. Penny left word with your mother. Then she called another doctor but he wouldn't come. Every time I tried to get up, I'd pass out. I couldn't get any air. When your dad got home, he came plowing down to my house, picked me up, threw me over his shoulder, put me in his car, drove me to the back of the hospital, took me up the ramp, threw me in bed, and hit me with adrenalin again. He was going to do a tracheotomy on me. Holly, his nurse, swabbed my throat where he was going to cut. I gave a big gasp and threw her halfway across the room. By the next morning, I was OK. But if your dad hadn't come over and gotten me, I'd have been dead."

Jim Bening, who had worked his way up from hardrock mining to resource management and then became a lumberman and finally a developer, was my father's friend and drinking and gambling buddy. He was warm and handsome in a western way with black hair and a broad face and smile, his arms strong and hands callused from his logging days. His speech was often rough, peppered with grammatical slips and swear words.

Once or twice a week, Jim met Dad for lunch at the Sunshine Inn. "An old beer molly—you know, who's been drunk—came up to your dad with her eye full of pus, saying 'I've got trouble with this eye.' Jesus Christ, he got up and babied and took care of her. Goddam shit running out of her eyes. She finally went away. I told Glen, 'I really enjoy having lunch with you, but this goddam idea of pus running out of her eye and I'm trying to eat soup, ain't goin' to work.' He said, 'You goddam big baby.' He was a hell of a lot of fun."

Sometimes, his nurse Janet said, one of the other doctors would stop at my father's office door and ask about a procedure. His response reminded the other doctor of a certain page of a textbook where the procedure was described. My father's memory was photographic.

If an operation was too delicate or a disease too complex, demanding more skills than any of the doctors in Kellogg possessed, my father sent a patient to specialists in Spokane, seventy miles away. Jim's young son was struck by a car. My father treated him first, stabilizing him and diagnosing brain damage he could not treat. He rode in the ambulance with the boy to Spokane. For weeks, the youngster teetered on the brink of death until he slowly began to recover. Jim told me later that if the boy had not been taken to Spokane so promptly, he would not have lived.

Bunker Hill medical coverage paid my father and the other doctors for all medical attention to the miners and their families. Bunker also owned the hospital, and my father and his four partners leased it. In 1958, Wardner Hospital was replaced by the West Shoshone General Hospital, built by the county at the opening of the gulch where the new high school was located. The doctors built their own clinic in Sunnyside. Both the old and new hospitals were always available to the whole community, as were the doctor services.

Everyone called my father "Doc." He delivered over five thousand babies, more than twice the population of the town that remains. Each doctor had a day "on call" and they rotated weekends. By and large, they worked well together, although my father sometimes resented the fact that he served more patients than any three of the others and so often worked harder and longer hours. Mondays, he said, were the hardest. Those were his on-call days. On

Mondays, all the older people, women especially, came down to the clinic to see him. They had endured lonely weekends and wanted company. Sometimes, he saw forty to sixty patients in a day, staying at the clinic and hospital until he finished with appointments and then making evening rounds. He worked twelve- and fourteen-hour days and never turned away anyone.

Another one of my father's jobs was the regular inspection of prostitutes to be certain they were disease-free—a twice-a-month duty. Prostitution was accepted and encouraged, as long as the "girls" were checked regularly for venereal disease. My friends didn't know about this aspect of his work, but because of it I always felt a secret affinity to the women in the "houses," which we passed every day going to and from the high school.

When my father and his partners weren't treating the town's ills, they played tricks on each other. Dad came home from a vacation to find his office turned into a gambling den with a rag doll "hooker" in a blonde wig, poker chips and cards strewn all over, overflowing ashtrays reeking with dead cigar butts, liquor bottles and an old slot machine. Another doctor, known for his habit of passing gas, found an outhouse in his office and a sign over the door: *BAROOOM!!* Still another once found his examining room set up as an operating room with a fake patient on the table and a string of wieners being pulled from the abdomen by a mannequin dressed in white and wearing steel-rimmed glasses. The tricksters delivered a load of rabbits to one doctor's house, two nanny goats to another, wild roosters to a third. An old disheveled raincoat made the rounds as a Christmas gift for a dozen years.

Music was almost as much a part of my father's world as medicine. He had been playing in a band since he was twelve years old. He helped finance his college education by playing the drums and leading a dance band at the University of Idaho. He played the piano, too, his right foot tapping out the beat: "Boogie Woogie Blues," "Sunny Side of the Street," songs he said reminded him of

Chicago and his medical school days, and "Sweet Georgia Brown." Mother bought him a drum set and placed it in the den at our summer place at Coeur d'Alene Lake. Many Friday evenings, he played wildly to the radio or to his own record collection of jazz.

Sometimes, I wonder if he missed not having a music career. He loved the night, loved the drums and jazz and blues and Big Band music. Rhythm flowed in his veins and rattled his bones. His hands and feet were hardly ever still, even when he sat in his big red chair in the den reading medical books. A pencil, his shoe, his hand, tapped out a beat.

It wasn't only in the hospital that patients approached my father. Wherever we went as a family, men and women waved to him, calling "Hey, Doc!" "How's your body?" he asked when they stopped by our table at a restaurant or talked to him on the street. Most people knew my father played drums at the Sunshine Inn. They knew he drank, but they also knew he didn't drink at work. His drinking began only when he returned home in the evening or when he was out at night and not on call.

Dead bodies must have often been in my father's daily life: cutting into them in medical school, closing their eyes in the wards and then telling families of loss. In the Sunshine Mine disaster where ninety-one miners died underground, my father took his turn at the top of the shaft when men were brought up, dead from smoke inhalation. Occasionally, I saw him red-eyed, but I was too young to know if it was from tears or drink.

When my father drank, he raged.

His partners were "pricks" and "mother-fuckers" because my father said he brought in three times as much as any other one doctor and earned only an equal share. He used his foul language on everyone. After a few drinks, he often worked himself into a temper tantrum over political issues—Castro taking over Cuba, the institution of "socialized medicine" via Medicare, the end of the gold standard, and taxes. He shouted, his voice hammering, and he sprinkled "damns" and "hells" and "fucks" in every sentence. The more he drank, the worse his words. He felt no compunction about calling and ranting to anyone. On a particularly bad night he called newly-elected President Kennedy to complain about Medicare. Not long after, the telephone company warned that if he continued to use language "like that," his telephone would be shut off.

My father used to call Bob Robson in the middle of the night, screaming. Bob answered, "You rotten s-o-b, you're drunk. Go to bed." People who couldn't handle my father would also call Bob. "I'd get up and get my pants on and go get him. Take him home, sit there and guard the door so he couldn't get out. I did it a lot of times. He saved my life once and I wouldn't forget that. He was a good friend and I did love him."

The other doctors, politicians, and even friends were not the only targets of my father's anger and foul language. Not immune were my mother, my brother, and finally, me.

None of us understood his sudden rages, the sarcasm that lay below the surface most of the time, his self-destructive binges. We hoped each time for the music side of him, the beat in his head and feet, and the gentle side of him, the careful touch for a sickness, a hurt, or even the jolly side of him, although it came most often after he'd been drinking—telling jokes, making bets, bragging about our accomplishments. We could never predict which mood, which side.

My brother, my sister, and I were always wary. He would laugh at a joke one minute and turn on our mother or on us the next, growing angry, shouting, yelling obscenities at her, accusing her of sneaking around behind his back. I wonder now if she thought she had stepped from the bad dream of her mother accusing her father of infidelity into the nightmare of being accused by my father of the same thing. Maybe Mother worried she too was paranoid, or maybe the seeds of doubt were planted about her father. Once he bloodied his hand breaking a wine glass. Another time, he broke a window in the back door. My brother tried to shout him down several times, trying to protect our mother, and was belted for his pain. He grabbed and pulled my hair more than once, but his physical acts were nothing compared to the verbal abuse.

My brother was "stupid, stupid, stupid." I was a "whore, a slut," or worse. I brought home a quarter grade of B+ in Chemistry and joined my brother in the stupid pile until I earned back an A by semester end. I didn't get a B again. Only my sister seemed to escape the words.

Did we ever let our guard down? I remember a trip to ski races in Spout Springs, Oregon. Dad took a group of us in our yellow Ford station wagon. We stayed at the lodge and—dressed in a plaid flannel shirt, dark pants, and regular shoes—he played Ping-Pong with everyone, raising the paddle, swatting the ball, grinning hugely. Before the race, he climbed up the hill, wearing galoshes with his pants tucked in and a dark blue jacket. He wore a knitted ski hat and looked out of his own character and alien to all the other parents who wore ski gear. He stood with two other parents holding stop watches. On the 4-3-2-1-GO, they all moved their hands up and down at the same time, clicking together on GO. When the skier passed the gates, they clicked again and compared times. Everybody seemed to like our dad. We did too, that time.

There was another side to him. He worked hard and expected us to do so too as students and musicians. He assumed we would attend college, make something of ourselves, and I never heard him limit our opportunities. I think he was disappointed none of us went to medical school. He helped with homework occasionally, but mostly, he was gone—at the clinic or hospital, out on house calls.

He took care of his patients, joked with them on the streets, knew everybody, knew their families, their kids, their aches, their pains, their likes and dislikes, even their joys. His nurse said he could walk into an exam room, not having seen a patient for six or seven years, and ask about the whole family, remember the earlier ills. He must have listened to them, asked them questions, expressed concern. Everybody in town knew him. I have never identified myself as his daughter without having someone say what a wonderful doctor he was, how he touched a life, many lives. What a character. What a drummer. What a doctor. No one ever said: What a drunk. They forgave him.

Unfortunately, my bad memories endure—his drinking, his smoking, his overeating, his contempt for his fellow doctors, his seemingly bottomless anger at us and our mother. My recurring image of him is with his mouth full of food, his cheeks ballooned, his lips pooched forward, saliva gathered in the corner of his mouth, food bits leaking out, his forehead slightly damp, his face red from drinking. Often he talked with food in his mouth in a loud, aggressive tone, swear words and vulgarisms salted throughout. I watched my plate a lot. But not every evening was spoiled with drink because often he planned to return to work to finish up paperwork or make evening rounds. Many nights, he studied in the den, listened to music, or sorted through his stamp collection, an occasional hobby since boyhood.

Did he want to be that way? Always, he seemed so frustrated with his life. Was being a doctor part of the difficulty? Maybe he knew so many ways of dying that he lived in fear of death. Maybe the night music he made kept the shadows away. Maybe his ability to comfort and to care, to patch and mend, lay uneasily with his inability to save *all* the patients who came to him for help. Sometimes, he appeared to be enjoying life. But then he drank and he seemed to spoil it for himself with his rages.

Whenever he grew weary of long hours at the hospital or of death and dying, whether from mine accidents, disease or design, he joined the poker tables at the Corner Club or sat in on the drums with Tommy's Trio at the Sunshine Inn. He played like a Gene Krupa, rattling on the snare drum, pinging on the high-hat double cymbals, whisking on the big cymbal, beating the bass with the pedal under his right foot, his hands moving rapidly. All the while he kept the beat with his tongue against his teeth, a *tata da, tata da, tata da* sound. The more he drank, the wilder he played, drumsticks a white blur, large pale blue eyes rolling and bloodshot, his face and hands melting into sound and rhythm.

Next morning, shaved and smelling of Old Spice, he downed a cup of coffee, gobbled a piece of toast, grabbed his stethoscope from his dresser, and dashed out the door, calling back, "See you later, alligator."

16

Look Out!

Football and basketball consumed the town. Our teams, the Wildcats, and their various members were the constant topic of conversation in stores, on the streets, around dinner tables, at parties. The adoration of the boys was not limited to high school girls. Everyone knew every team member. Everyone attended the ball games, whether outside in a driving snowstorm or inside under the lights.

The Damiano boys, Rollie Williams, George White, Rich Porter, Bernard Blondeau, Bohunk Dejanovich, Jack Morbeck, Rich Edwards. Over the years a pantheon of boys played ball for Kellogg and often went on to the University of Idaho to play ball there too. Our basketball team won the state AAA high school championship two out of five years during my junior high and high school days. Half the town followed them to games in Spokane, Coeur d'Alene, Sandpoint, Wallace, and finally to the championship series in Boise, the state capital. Purple-and-gold letter sweaters symbolized heroic status.

The social life of teenagers wound around the sports events: dances after games, bonfires before games, formal proms planned when no sporting events were scheduled. The high school marching band for football and pep band for basketball played at all home games and often traveled with the team for away games.

Being in the band didn't have quite the cachet of team members, but those of us who played believed we helped win.

Surely all small towns make the same claims, behave the same way. Because our town sat in the Bitterroot Mountains, however, we had an additional claim to fame. Our ski team.

Lookout Pass, Idaho, was where we learned to ski. I always liked the sound of the name and loved the place. Look out! We skied at breakneck speed, the wind in our faces, turning here, turning there, swiveling our hips, and stopping with an uphill christie and a wave of snow.

And look out over the mountains below. From the top, we surveyed our known world, west toward Mullan and Wallace and Kellogg, and east to distant white peaks and St. Regis, Saltese, and Silver Dollar—miles into Montana, covered as far as the eye could see with snowy peaks and deep-green forests sheltering cougars and grizzly bears. Then down we swooped. Get out of our way! We're fast, we're neat, watch us go and marvel at our skill, our goggled eyes, our slick skis and boots, our ski belts worn low like six-shooters.

The only thing that spoils this image of our former selves are the actual moving pictures my mother took. We look young, sometimes awkward, crouched in funny positions, and not fast at all. It has to be the fault of the old-fashioned film. We were gladiators and speed kings. We were warriors. Look out!!

Our ski-racing team, including skiers from Mullan, Wallace, and Kellogg, traveled on weekends in winter, leaving town on a Thursday, just like football and basketball players, to race at White Pass or Spout Springs or Mount Spokane. No school sports for girls existed, although occasionally in P.E. we played basketball—six to a team, with three on one side of the center line and three on the other, a line we could not cross. Girls' Rules. In skiing, boys and girls raced separately, but used the same courses.

Skiing was central to the life of many Kellogg children and teens. In the early years, unlike today, skiing was pretty much available to anyone in our valley. Ski equipment and clothing were handed down from family to family, from older child to younger child, from neighbor to neighbor. Ski lessons and bus transportation to the mountain were free, both paid for by the United Crusade (now United Way) organization and by Bunker Hill. Tickets to ski were fifty cents, seventy-five cents, then one dollar.

My brother and I took the bus every Saturday morning. Along with 150 other kids, we crowded alongside the yellow ski buses, holding our skis up, curved tips first. A pair at a time, the drivers on top grabbed and stacked them in boxes. They tied a canvas cover over the jumble, clambered down, climbed into the bus, swung the door closed, put each bus in gear—the engines were already going—and off we went to Lookout Pass.

Up the road along the river to Wallace, two turns in Wallace and then up the beginning grade to Mullan we traveled, singing. "Working on the Railroad," "Daisy," "K-K-K-Katie," and "99 Bottles of Beer on the Wall." At Mullan we passed the Morning Mine, its red buildings stair-stepping down the mountainside, one of the oldest operations along with Bunker Hill in the Idaho Panhandle. Always, there was snow everywhere. At Lookout Pass, we waited for our skis to be handed down, pair by pair.

The earliest skis had bear-trap bindings with long straps to wrap three or four times around the boot, holding them in place come hell or high water, ice or deep snow, and broken ankles. My first "real" skis, a pair with edges, narrow metal pieces screwed along both bottom edges of the skis, were Gresvigs with Marker cable bindings. With cables, the strap only wrapped around the boot once. We carried bamboo poles with big baskets. Eventually, the skis were metal or fiberglass, the bindings complicated but safer, the poles aluminum and the baskets plastic. We wore leather boots with square toes and laces. They were large and heavy compared to shoes but minuscule beside modern boots, hard plastic with metal buckles, encasing our feet and legs halfway to our knees.

The log lodge straddled the Idaho-Montana state line. Such a steamy, wool-smelling, slick-floored, noisy, wonderful place. Our ski hill was three rope tows high, a little over 1,100 vertical feet. To ride up, we used rope-tow holders, clamps, and later hooks that clung to the rope. Both kinds connected with a heavy cord to the webbed belt around our waists. The ropes were thick, an inch or so, and ran on pulleys with a safety gate at the end. We told gory stories to each other of being tangled in the rope, pulled over the gate, and into the pulley where our heads would be split in two.

When there was new snow, the whole ski school went up the first lift, spread out in a line and sidestepped down to pack the snow. This would be sacrilege now; powdered snow is all, but now our skis are shorter and wider, too. As our lessons advanced, we moved up to the other lifts to ski and to race. One test was to ski from top to bottom as fast as we could. Wind whipped my face and my jacket rattled and nothing else made me feel quite so free and strong.

Art Audette, the ski school head, race director, and swimming coach in the summer, taught us to ski, moving from one class to another all day. A lesson imprinted in all of us by a thousand iterations over the course of a whole winter was the "wind up." Turn the body up-hill, left hand at the left back pocket, then unwind the other way, and our long, long skis would turn. We advanced from snowplow to stem turn to christie, a turn keeping the skis parallel.

Tall and tanned, Art was graced with sea-blue eyes and long dark lashes that would attract the flintiest of women, let alone a shy, book-involved youngster like me. Burnished gold curls, thick chest hair, and rippling muscles (seen in the swimming pool) made him irresistible. For him, we would swim fifty laps of the pool in one session, boot-pack a slalom and giant slalom course in a single morning, practice gates until it was too dark to see, save a "drowning" victim over and over. There were no Girls Rules for Art. He expected as much from us as from the boys, was as pleased when we won and as disappointed when a girl fell as when a boy did; he handed out medals to girls with dash and aplomb. We were a ski *team*.

Races filled one or two weekends a month—slalom first day, downhill second. We received our race numbers the first morning and wore them as badges of courage all weekend. I won medals, not as many as I wanted, but enough to want to be an Olympic skier. In the eighth-grade P.E., I announced my plans to ski in the 1964 Olympics. Several Olympic skiers did come from Lookout Pass: Jim Barrier, Big Eyes Bennett, and Beverly Anderson. Winning was important, but second or third wasn't bad. I found the bronze medals had the same heft as the "gold."

"Oh, yes," I say, "I used to race." The glamour I try to infuse in those words is a lie; I felt glamorous and at ease only after the awarding of the medals in the lodge. But the competition was real, a first lesson in the lessons of living. And one I can remember without the stress that accompanied so many other lessons learned since I stopped racing to face other challenges, mostly greater in the eyes of others, but often lesser in my own heart. My early skiing competition now seems as remote as a forgotten lifetime to me, but I still love to ski, fast and hard. And when I'm skiing, I once again recapture that sense of being a hero. I feel my body's strength and the self-confidence and the freedom I knew as a fourteen-year-old girl. Art Audette gave that gift to everyone he coached.

17

Strive for Perfection!
Play with Feeling!

Cultural activities, although limited, did exist in Kellogg, primarily in the community concert series. Four times a year, musicians came to Kellogg—pianists, harpists, violinists, flutists, chamber quartets, singers. The concerts played in the high school gym with folding chairs set up on the gym floor before a stage dais. Lots of people attended—men in suits, women and girls in their "good" or "church" clothes. We picked up printed programs and muted our voices until all were seated and a waiting hush settled over the audience, much as in church. Then the musicians appeared—women in long somber dresses, men in black ties and tuxedos or dark suits. We all listened politely, checking the programs for names of the songs, often not all that familiar, at least to me, except by the name of the composer.

I wonder what the musicians thought: stacks belching clouds of smoke and things no one wanted to know about, treeless hillsides, burnt grass in summer and dirty snow in winter, a high school gym with poor acoustics, and a scrubbed audience that for all they knew could barely appreciate the music. I doubt if they realized that at least part of the audience had graduated from universities around the country or traveled the world and lived among other cultures and societies. The audience always clapped enthusiastically, giving standing ovations every time, and eliciting as many encores as possible.

As Dolly Parker pointed out, Kellogg was a whirl of dances, dinners, parties. My parents attended nearly everything, including three Kellogg-Wallace formal dances each year. The men wore tuxes and the women long formal dresses. Live bands played while everyone danced all evening at the Elks Club in Wallace or the Union-Legion Hall in Kellogg. Small groups met for cocktails before the dances and for oyster stew or other repast after the dances. Those pre- and post-functions grew in size and in alcohol imbibed until finally the dances ended due to nominal attendance. Each week in the summer, my parents attended a potluck dinner at the golf course, although neither played golf, and danced afterwards. The Bunker Hill Staff House was also the scene of special teas, wedding receptions, Christmas parties for businesses, including the hospital.

My mother loved dresses that flared when my father twirled her on the dance floor. She was lovely in her evening clothes: a bright-red taffeta dress, waltz-length, with bright red lipstick to match. A white dress with fringes from top to bottom. A blue crepe with a swirly skirt, blue earrings and necklace and matching shoes. Her hair was curled and she always smelled perfume-y with feminine smells, not kitchen-y with ammonia or floor-wax smells. She must have powdered herself and then splashed on Chanel or White Shoulders. Even Mom's lipstick smelled good.

Dad dressed in a suit and tie on those party nights, fat already but not bad-looking before he drank too much. With two martinis or two Scotches, his whole face seemed to melt like wax. Dad's favorite television show was *The Honeymooners*, perhaps because he bore a striking resemblance to Jackie Gleason, not only physically, but emotionally—quick anger, flaring tantrum, deep regret.

Most of Mother's clothes came from Donna's on McKinley

Avenue, two doors from the corner with Main. Donna's clothes always smelled good too. In the display window were mannequins all dolled up, and piles of gorgeous sweaters and a rainbow of colorful Jantzen knit outfits. When the door opened, a bell jingled, and Donna, her fingers all rings and garlanded with necklaces and bracelets on her arms, greeted everyone. She was slightly pudgy, with short black hair, sparkled glass frames, a deep tan, and lots of eye make-up, smelling like cinnamon. While she served a customer, showing off new arrivals and helping to fit clothes in the dressing room, her chatter flowed with news and gossip, about her clothes, other people, events, business. What Mother didn't buy for herself, my father bought at Christmas and on her birthday— lacy lingerie and fluffy peignoir sets.

In fancy high heels, sparkling or color-banded in satin, Mom reached to Dad's shoulders and they were a handsome pair for the brief leave-taking from our house. They swept around the dance floor, laughing and happy together, mother's feet light and flashing, twinkle toes. As heavy as my father was, he was light on his feet. The few times I danced with him, I couldn't follow his lead because his steps were too complicated.

The other cultural events grew out of school activities: school plays and spring concerts. One of the most influential people in town was our school's music director.

In Kellogg, anyone who wanted to could take band. Either the school or the director, Glenn Exum, would be sure we all had instruments. The only criteria for getting into and staying in the band was a commitment to practicing and performing.

The summer following the fourth grade, I took up the flute. Each time I opened the case, I felt a rush of surprise and pleasure to see my polished silver instrument separated into parts and nestled in blue velvet. Magic exuded from the metallic smell that leaped out, slightly bitter and cold. Within days, I knew my hands and mouth would delight in this instrument. What I did not know was that my band teacher would rule my days and shape my life.

Mr. Exum explained how the instruments worked and how to elicit mellow sounds. With one of our instruments, he would demonstrate where to place arched fingers, how to stand or sit. Breathing came high on the list. Sit straight, shoulders back, breathe from the diaphragm, a section of the body unknown to all of us until then. Like an eagle, he watched our shoulders, ready to pounce if they lifted.

In the fall, we met daily after classes and the warm friendliness changed to the beginning drumbeats of the search for perfection. Mr. Exum demanded that we practice an hour a day, which with my piano practice, also an hour, and my studies, left precious little time for other activities. In junior high, if we were good enough players, we were invited to join senior band, which met every morning at the high school.

Glenn Exum spent his summers climbing the Teton Mountains in Wyoming. At seventeen, he reached the top of the Grand Teton on a never-before-climbed route, thence forward called the Exum Route. He taught climbing, took others on climbs, and established the Exum Climbing School in Jackson. If we knew this as kids, it was only a vague knowledge that he did something else, something grown-up. The climbing must have renewed his engine because he came back in the fall, eager and demanding as usual.

Tall and dressed in pants with a knife-edge crease and a starched shirt and bowtie, his bald head circled by a short dark fringe of hair, Mr. Exum goaded us to perfection—challenging, pleading, berating, scolding. With spittle flying, he exhorted everyone and praised those who responded.

"No, no, no, no! Listen to yourself! Your instrument sounds like a sick bull," he scolded the first trombone. "This is not a song for caterwauling cats!" he accused the clarinets. "Sing! That phrase should sing! Each note should flow into the next. Play with *feeling!*" His arms flowed back and forth and up and down. He rapped the podium with his baton. "Don't breathe in the middle!" he ordered. "Clean, crisp, clear. *This* is what it should sound like." He grabbed the trumpet from first chair and played—cleanly, crisply, and clearly.

Many days, we played up to his expectations. The John Phillip Sousa marches stirred my feet and my heart. And school fight songs, cribbed from colleges around the country, made me believe if I played just right, our team would win. I loved the trumpets, because they brought images of jousting matches and cavalry charges. The saxophone crooned low, sultry notes, pulling at stones inside me.

We struggled with light classical music, such as the Poet and Peasant Overture by von Suppe or the L'Arlasienne Suite by Bizet. We played Tchaikovsky, Dvorak, MacDowell, and Gershwin. More than once, we listened to solos or group sections that were indeed played with feeling, and we left the band room humming the melodies. Because we had no stringed instruments, the notation for band music substituted clarinets or flutes for violin parts.

At my best, my flute trilled rippling notes, summer water flowing in green meadows—an image from a book, not from our town. At my worst, the notes were breathy and slow, but still added oomph to the band. As part of this larger enterprise of sound and beauty, I lost my shyness and often played solos. If I practiced and played well, I earned rewards: satisfied smiles on Mr. Exum's face, pleasure for myself, and first chair.

* * *

Monday was competition day. Alan, a plump, pale-skinned fellow flute player who usually played second chair to my first, raised his hand. When he did, the other instrument sections relaxed. The challenger selected the piece and played first. Alan always performed with mathematical precision. Then I lifted my flute with trembling hands. I knew my face was flushed; heat surrounded me like a halo. I played the same piece, but with *feeling*. If I had practiced the piece, I could relax half a breath. If I had not, the heel of my foot shook.

I can still see Mr. Exum rubbing his hands together in satisfaction, and when I wasn't the target, I felt the same. Not only did we hear displays of truly expert skill and musicality, we ourselves voted up or down by clapping, a small touch of the Roman circus, determining the order of chairs—first, second, third, and so on.

While the rest of the band decided our fate, Alan smirked his round face and cupid's-bow mouth. His short black hair bristled. He always expected perfection to win. Occasionally, it did. As often as not, however, the band members clapped on whim. Sometimes I played poorly and won. If I did lose, Alan promptly moved into my place, plopping his bottom onto the first metal folding chair, grabbing and settling his music in place of mine. The next week I raised my hand to challenge him and regain my rightful place.

Pep band, concert band, band practice. Each morning we met—in the snowy chill of winter before dawn; in fall and spring as the sun was rising above the barren mountains that enclosed our Idaho valley. Each morning, too, Mr. Exum lectured us briefly on some quality he considered of value: honesty, integrity, hard work, clear minds, clean living, the outdoors, community concerts, egalitarianism, patriotism. Although we may have rolled our eyes, we listened, and then turned to our music.

We marched in parades, played at music festivals and concerts. Gold stripe on our legs and gold braid on our chests decorated the purple uniforms, designed for broad-chested, long-legged boys. The brimmed hat with a gold plume sank almost to my nose. Stuffed with paper, the hat stopped at eyebrow level. I felt small, skinny, ugly, and top-heavy.

We performed intricate drills on the street and on the football field. But first we practiced, practiced, practiced. Perfection always was Mr. Exum's star. We memorized our music—no fluttering pages and music holders on our instruments when we marched in public. The precision of the band gave me a sense of order. Each row must be straight—side to side and back to front.

Next to us in parades and at football games strutted members of the drill team, girls with fitted tops, short skirts, white boots, and twirling purple and gold flags. The contrast with the band members was freedom to bondage; beauty to utility; and finally, female to male. I began to yearn for some of that freedom and beauty.

The whole town attended our spring extravaganzas. Themes for the concerts changed from year to year and we all wore costumes. Whether our music related to an Irish spring, a minstrel show, the sights and sounds of New York City, or the fairly new medium of television, everyone joined us. We worked on songs and skits, overtures and popular songs, presenting revues that took us away from spring dreariness of the treeless mountains around us to other worlds and other cultures.

Every year, we played a major orchestral work. This piece was always the grand finale of our own Spring Concert, and our entry into the competition at the Lewiston Music Festival. My sophomore year, Mr. Exum selected the William Tell Overture, better known, then, as the Lone Ranger theme on television. The flute part was intricate with fast fingering for notes up and down the scale from the highest A to the lowest C. I practiced until my mouth was sore. We rehearsed until the band was exhausted. The one respite, the one reward each week was . . . no flute competition. Only one could play this solo. A change from week to week would, in Mr. Exum's opinion, weaken the whole band.

"Strive for perfection! Play with feeling!" he told me. "Play as you have never played before," he exhorted the band. Once, I forgot my music. He ranted about my disloyalty, my sloppy habits, my gross negligence, until I was in tears. I did not forget my music again.

The festival took place for four days every April. We traveled by bus from Kellogg, leaving dead snow, dead trees, dead streets filled with mud and grit, and dead air, to springtime in Lewiston. Daffodils, red and pink tulips, purple and white lilacs. The only drawbacks were the pulp mill smell, its rotten-egg aroma worse than our smelter smoke, and our collective stage fright. The two are forever linked in my memory. Even lilacs couldn't overpower sulfur and fear.

On the last night of the festival, we sat on stage, dressed in white shirts and navy blue pants or skirts, our instruments polished and ready, our music, the William Tell Overture, in order. Mr. Exum came to the podium, his face fixed in a tight smile. He raised his hands. We lifted our instruments with one motion. His arms fell and rose twice while he counted, "Uh one, uh two." On the third downstroke we began. His mustache wiggled up and down, his lips pursed. He grimaced and smiled; his eyes sought each of us out and instructed and ordered in the same glance to concentrate, to play with feeling. The top of his head gleamed in the concert lights and tiny drops of perspiration formed as he drew music from us and our instruments.

William Tell galloped. The trumpets charged; the clarinets played in unison; the trombones thundered; the timpani rumbled. My fingers flew over the keys and my notes soared along an arpeggio of melody. I breathed in all the right spots, at one with the musical score. My solo was perfection itself. Even I knew it. At the end, Mr. Exum bowed to the band. He turned to me, and bowed again. I was triumphant, and briefly, it didn't matter if I looked like a boy in my uniform.

Of course we won the blue ribbon. Our band—Mr. Exum's band—was the best! We always won blue. Any less would have been an embarrassment for him and, more importantly, for us. His high standards were now ours.

Was the glory of our blue ribbon, the audience clapping, our playing worth all the early morning band practices, the late evening instrument practices, the tears and anger before competition, the trembling knees and sometimes sick stomachs, the scratchy uniforms, and the occasional dripping sarcasm of Mr. Exum? Yes. At that moment, when we stood with the lift of Mr. Exum's hands, yes it was. Now, in my memory, it was, and then, in real time, it was.

* * *

On the last day of school that spring, I went to Mr. Exum's office, quaking in my shoes. I had finally persuaded my parents that I should quit playing the flute and concentrate on piano instead. My parents consented, but only if I had the courage to tell Mr. Exum myself.

"No one who has quit band has ever made anything of himself," he said, his face lined in a deep frown. "It is a sign of laziness and lack of self-discipline."

What could I say? I rarely responded to my father's harangues. I couldn't bring myself to argue with Mr. Exum because, in part, I believed him.

"How can your parents permit you to do this? You have such promise. You have a challenge to live up to. How can you let this opportunity go by? You'll be sorry."

I put away my flute because I wanted to join the drill team. Why? To be a girl. The lure of boys and dates seduced me away from music. I would march again, this time twirling a rippling flag, wearing cunning white boots with swinging tassels. Now I too would strut and swing my hips and smile and flash my eyes at the crowds. I too would shake my hair and garner smiles from boys. Excellence and intelligence didn't matter. I wanted to be pretty.

18
It's All in the Game

Maybe because all the timber in the area went into the mines, all our schools were brick—several grade schools, a junior high, and a high school. My brick elementary schoolhouse sat down the street from my house, a short walk there and back and home at lunch. All our grade-school teachers were women, both married and unmarried: Mrs. Moore, Mrs. Sawyer, Mrs. Harratt, Mrs. Jones, Mrs. Popov, and Miss Lindberg, the principal as well as sixth-grade teacher. Their husbands were connected to mining, either working at the Bunker office building, as mining engineers, or in the case of Mrs. Jones, a union leader. Not that I knew any of their husbands.

Every day began with the Pledge of Allegiance. No Bible reading in our schools. School was easy for me and I loved excelling at it—answering a question or spelling a word, preparing outlines of American history and reports on Aztecs or the state of Florida or a book I'd read, completely filling in book wheels with colored pencils to show how many books I'd finished, doing arithmetic problems in neat rows, winning long-division races at the blackboard, turning in extra homework. I hated to leave school. At home was an unpredictable father I was scared of and who drank. Outside were kids who called me "Bones" and "Skinny." My revenge and my solace were to outdo everyone in the classroom. I loved my teachers and they loved me—the good little student and teacher's pet.

Miss Lindberg, who taught sixth grade with Mrs. Popov, set the standard for all my teachers to come. Miss Lindberg wore makeup —red rouge, eyebrow pencil, mascara, and red lipstick—something not many women in our town did. Her many necklaces and bracelets clinked and clanked with fake stones and fake gold and flashed when she moved her arms and hands. Rings studded both hands with big colorful stones to match her clothes and to emphasize her long painted red nails. Those hands expressed her—always in motion, pointing, emphasizing, describing, gesturing. Her voice, too, was emphatic. On the mantel of my house is a lipstick plant—all green with blood-red flowers—and it reminds me of Miss Lindberg. Her clothes were as bright as the rest of her, but well-tailored and possibly expensive. In class she wore a loose smocklike top, like an artist's jacket. Very stylish, we girls thought.

One of my friends has told me that Miss Lindberg was the first teacher who made her feel like a real person, capable and intelligent, personable and worth something. Miss Lindberg's unique quality, I think, was to make all of us feel cherished. When we met her standards, as she expected each of us to do, she exclaimed and complimented, as if we had achieved great heights.

By the fourth grade we carried homework home each night, along with a stack of books. The stacks grew higher and heavier as we advanced to junior high and high school. Our classes differed little, I imagine, from classes today: arithmetic and then mathematics, English literature and writing, science and then biology and chemistry, history of Idaho and the United States and the world, social studies and civics. We memorized, outlined, created topographic salt maps, wrote papers, computed page after page of math problems, prepared special projects about other cultures, and learned about the world outside our valley as well as studied art, music, drama, debate, and journalism.

* * *

When I reached seventh grade, our whole class, as well as the seventh-grade students from Sunnyside, Smelterville, and Pinehurst, were sent as a group to an abandoned high school in Kingston, about seven miles from Kellogg. The new high school was under construction in Kellogg, and the rest of the grades eight through twelve were crammed into the old one. Initially, the bus ride out of town to the old brick structure next to marshlands seemed a sentence to Siberia. Our isolation created a huge bond between students from all walks of life and all locations in the mining valley.

Everyone bused, so there was no stigma attached to riding a bus. We all did it. The bus ride itself, perhaps twenty minutes, allowed us to do last-minute homework, catch up on gossip learned in long telephone calls the night before, get to know a different set of girls and boys, and plan activities—dances, skating parties, ski Saturdays, basketball and football cheering sections. A new world of potential boyfriends opened.

The school itself was isolated in a marsh with cattails, frogs, birds, insects and creepy critters, many of which the boys caught and used to chase the girls. That year served as a transition from childhood to adolescence, perhaps allowing us extra time in the former while getting used to the latter. This was the year we first moved from class to class, teacher to teacher. Mrs. Williams for social studies, Miss Batts for English, Mrs. Riley for P.E., and others. Bells rang and we shuffled through creaking halls still smelling of fresh paint, or out into the schoolyard for activities. This was the year we learned to pick teams the old-fashioned way—strongest and best first, weakest and unpopular last. I often was last. This was the year other students poked fun at my good grades rather than admiring my abilities.

This was the year my school photo appeared to be all nose and oily hair and tell-tale signs of pimples. This was the year I grew hair under my arms and cut it with cuticle scissors. And, worst of all, this was the year I discovered every other girl in the universe wore a bra. I did not. My mother insisted I didn't need one. The change room for physical education was a constant embarrassment. I tried to don my undershirt quickly and hoped others would mistake the lines under my blouse for a bra. When the boys chased the girls to snap bras, I hid. My worst fear in the world was that a boy would discover that I didn't wear one! Then the whole world would know and laugh at me.

But this was also the year I made friends with a group of girls who remained close all through junior high and high school, who rallied to each other when in need, who wrote notes, talked on the telephone all hours, and worked together on school projects and played together in out-of-school activities. Even now, many of us remain close in spirit, if not in location. Without our shared year apart, I don't think this phenomenon would have happened. Our clique, as many would call it, contained most of the girls our age. Our fathers worked in hard rock mining, as smeltermen and in other mining jobs, in blue and white collar jobs, and in the professions. Some of our mothers worked; most did not. It didn't matter. We became a family of sorts, getting the kind of adolescent understanding that parents rarely give. Nor did we engage often in the usual back-biting, gossipy, petty activities of some girls. When I did finally leave home, I think one of the things I missed most, and it took me years to find again, was the supportive, close friendship of girls. Over a period of time, the entire year of my seventh grade has become in my memory a kind of lost year, but lost in a good sense, like the lost boys in *Peter Pan*.

* * *

Eighth-grade science class met in the basement of the former high school, a three-story brick building. (We were back in town from our banishment in seventh grade.) Our desks were the old-fashioned kind—rows of separate seats with flat-topped boxes, open in front to slide books and papers into, with attached one-person benches. The chalkboards were still black, the floors wood and varnished and smelling of wax every Monday morning. Along one wall, cupboards with windows contained beakers, rubber tubing, scales, dusty jars with strange shapes floating in formaldehyde, perhaps even a Bunsen burner or two—remnants of the former chemistry class, now removed to our brand-new steel and glass high school across town. Textbooks contained rudimentary drawings of radios with vacuum tubes, electric switches, fulcrums, levers and pulleys, our introduction to physics, another class waiting for us in high-school-land.

President Eisenhower had called the nation to educate more scientists, more engineers. Our teacher, Mr. Johnson, a slight but perfectly formed man, with delicate hands to match his slender body, took this call to science seriously. He felt charged, I am sure, with the very honor of his profession to bring our lagging sensibilities into the Cold War threat posed by Russia, and he was excited about our country's possibilities. He rarely stood at the front of the classroom to lecture. Rather, he liked to sit on top of a student's desk, placing his head several feet above ours. He selected an empty place and perched on the burnished, pocketknife-marked wood and swung one leg, sometimes balancing on the other, sometimes sitting back far enough so neither foot touched the floor.

He wore blue or red or green open-collared short-sleeve shirts on the warm days of early fall, and changed to plaid flannel shirts, buttoned not quite to his neck, as the days grew colder. Sometimes he rolled his sleeves, his "let's get to work" gesture, revealing strong, black-haired forearms. They fascinated me and I wondered whether Mr. Johnson's arm hair was soft like rabbit fur or wiry like horse hair. My own father had a practically hairless body—nothing on chest, arms, or legs—so Mr. Johnson seemed to be the epitome of masculinity.

I have no idea what we actually did in our science class—we hadn't yet had algebra or geometry, let alone calculus or physics. Biology was yet to come and chemistry a couple of years away. Our science book had lots of pictures and read a little like our history books—narrative with dates to remember, current to perhaps 1950.

But our teacher was too late. Our country was too late.

The next year, in 1957, Russia launched *Sputnik*, the first man-made item to be slung into an orbit around the earth. The world was electrified. Because this was a time deep in the Cold War, Americans, and especially the people in my world, were also terrified. If the USSR could do this, couldn't it also send bombs to blow us up, send out orbiting missiles to attack us at any time? The headlines in the *Kellogg Evening News* blared blackly at us: USSR Wins Space War. Such a humiliating admission: anonymous fat people in a backward country could outstrip the modern technology of our brainiest scientists and most advanced mathematicians.

Suddenly Senator McCarthy's hue and cry earlier about Communists in our government seemed likely. Our enemies were surrounding us, threatening us, perhaps eating away at us from the interior, like worms in wood. And what seemed worst of all, we were unprepared, according to the men with serious faces on television and some of our local teachers. Our scientists had failed us because our schools had failed us. The only way to fight the threat from the outside and from the inside was to educate our children better, including me in junior high in Kellogg, Idaho, and quickly too.

A call to arms went out to all states: Prepare!

We must get our own beeping satellite into orbit, aim our missiles at *them*, our president warned. We were too complacent, too uneducated, too backward, too naive, all the grownups in our lives complained. Turn our students' heads to science, science, science, something Mr. Johnson had urged a year earlier. Everyone except my mother said to forget art and music, and to spend less time on English and history. She even argued with my father at the dinner table, saying these subjects couldn't be ignored. He disagreed, often loudly and vulgarly. He, like so many others, said we must turn our attention to math, chemistry, physics. *Sputnik* entered our vocabulary with one giant headline and remained on our tongues for weeks and months.

On television we watched *Mickey Mouse Club* and *American Bandstand* and the *Adventures of Rin Tin Tin*. Science fiction shows, our staple when our new television first arrived at our house, had been our sole education about space, except for those of us who read. Edgar Rice Burroughs introduced me to Mars, to bodiless heads and aliens.

We no longer played Indian on the hill behind our house. But our play didn't turn to spaceships or secret chemical experiments in our basements. Probably nothing short of a revolution would have turned our attention from junior high basketball, band and drill team, Green Rivers and sodas at the drugstore after school, monthly dances at the gym, or the Sadie Hawkins Day dance where girls asked boys and we all dressed up like hillbillies. We danced to the strains of a live combo composed of drums, piano, and sax played by our principal, Mr. Woodbury, his wife and his son, and to songs like "Sentimental Journey," "Stardust," "Harvest Moon." But even those sensibilities were changing. On record nights, we rock 'n rolled to Bill Haley and the Comets and "Rock Around the Clock," as well as to Elvis and "Jailhouse Rock," "Blue Suede Shoes," and "Love Me Tender." Which records we owned carried far more impact in our lives than which scientific theorem might apply to the space race.

Our state decided our schools must improve. Because the system was locally controlled—no federal money in those days—our school board met, pictured for us to see in black and white photos in the newspaper, and carried on lengthy discussions. Eight dour men peering at the camera, the gravity of our lack of dedication to science weighing down their expressions. Our system did begin to change. The board adopted two tracks—one accelerated for those bound for college, one vocational for those headed into the mines, the woods, and into hands-on labor such as carpentry, plumbing, electricity.

I don't think girls entered anyone's mind in those discussions, although earlier Mr. Johnson had pointed out that everyone, girls included, must learn science. The school board still insisted, however, that girls take home economics, a required course, and often girls participated in the accelerated track only if their parents insisted. Most girls were directed to typing, bookkeeping, shorthand —all basic skills classes—and girls' clubs centered around occupations for women: Future Nurses, Teachers and Homemakers of America. Fortunately for me, my parents enrolled me in the accelerated courses beginning in high school.

After *Sputnik*, all our teachers and maybe a few of us students brooded about our humiliation as a twentieth-century marvel and our failures as scientists. My own earlier dreams of being the first woman on Mars, generated in part by books, the movie *Red Planet Mars*, and by Flash Gordon and Dr. Ming on television, struck me as childish by then. Nevertheless, amid speculation about what the Russians would do next, what we would do next, about spy satellites possibly already circling the globe, about Vanguards and ICBMs, I dreamed those dreams again.

The same year that Mr. Johnson excited us about science and maybe reaching the planets and the stars, Mrs. Cossey, girls' physical education teacher, taught dancing in class—tango, foxtrot, jitterbug (which we all thought we could do anyway), Charleston, and waltz. She advised our drill team, who, dressed as Scottish highlanders, marched in the Lilac Parade in Spokane, a first for our junior high. She also taught girls' health education classes, including basic sex education. For the first time, most of us girls learned the official names of our genitals and those of the boys, about the hormonal changes we were going through, basic hygiene, and something about sexual relations.

*   *   *

Unfortunately, a classmate's parents didn't approve. After one of our classes, a drawing of male genitalia was left on the blackboard and seen by the boys' health class. One of the boys, a neighbor of mine who played kissing games with all of us on summer evenings, told his parents. His mother marched down to the school and demanded Mrs. Cossey be fired. She was. This was the first example of the small-mindedness of our community of which I was aware. More would come.

It wasn't until I was in high school that the repercussions of firing Mrs. Cossey revealed themselves in our class. Our parents undoubtedly believed they would and should be responsible for their children's sex educations, a responsibility few of them fulfilled. The only "discussion" about sex in our house came from a small booklet my mother gave to me explaining—via the use of birds, animals, and bees—how humans propagated. The actual details I had learned several years earlier from a neighbor girl. The booklet also explained what menstruation was without using the word "blood." Unfortunately, I learned little and neither did quite a few of my friends and acquaintances.

*   *   *

During my sophomore year at Kellogg High School, my friend Betty arranged a blind date for me with one of the seniors. We went to a movie and then for Cokes at the Boat Drive-In and on to a parking spot up Vergobbi Gulch. Nothing about the date was remarkable except that I laughed a lot and I was out with an "older" man.

Tom and I doubled with Betty and her friend several times and then we went out alone in his car. He drove a shiny black car with gold striping and upholstered interior difficult to slip across, one of those round old-time cars that show up in gangster movies. All through the late fall and into winter, Tom continued to call and take me out—to football games, to Friday night dances, once in a while to dinner, to movies, to park. Sometimes, he gave me rides home from school. It felt delicious to have a boy/man pay attention to me, tell me how pretty I looked, to kiss and hold me, to meet me by my locker at school, touch my arm or back with his hand, and take me to formal dances. Few males had paid any kind of positive attention to me, except my band instructor and my ski coach. And I'd already quit band. Before long, I quit skiing too because Tom didn't ski.

I began to feel as if I had a "steady," something I already knew was forbidden in my house. No steadies. My brother had married in a shotgun wedding just a month or so after he turned seventeen. I was fourteen at the time. My father had raged around the house regularly ever since, making it clear that I could not have steady boyfriends, as I was certain to get "knocked up" (his parlance). The issue had not come up until I began dating Tom, but then it came up perhaps once a week, finally culminating in a direct order not to date him any more.

What to do? We weren't, in fact, going steady, although I made certain I was available for dates with him (not that my door was being beat down by other suitors). While I was struggling with how to handle this, what I should say to this "older" man without sounding like a child and what I should say to my father and mother, Tom dropped me.

The combination of forbidden fruit and being spurned turned what was probably gratitude for attention and puppy love into full-blown throbbing heartachy love. This kind of story was one my friends thrived upon, both for themselves and for me. Every morning, our group of girls met in the cafeteria to gossip; every noon we sat around a table in the cafeteria and gossiped some more. Every morning, noon, and every night on the telephone, I pined for Tom to my girlfriends. Betty and I played sad records for hours when we slept over at each other's house.

Nearly all of these friends I'd met in the seventh grade at Kingston. We stayed together through high school, with a few exceptions. One went away to a private school, two others moved to Washington, D.C. We were companions and soul mates. Betty Lou, Mannie (Mary Ann), Sylvia, Patti, Gayle, Diane, Ruthie, Renie, Marjeane, Carrie, Connie, Ellen, Wanda, Hazel, Jan, Judy, Penny, Karen, Carol, Bonnie, and others.

Blossoms of full skirts and petticoats in spring, a garden of colors in Jantzen outfits in the winter. We wore Jantzen skirts and sweaters, all one color, with matching socks. I had blue suede shoes, just as in the song. All the songs in our high school years seemed to be for me, for us, told of our lives in high school, in Kellogg, Idaho. "Going to Kansas City" was about going to basketball and football games in Coeur d'Alene, thirty miles down the road, and finding and flirting with cute boys. "It's All in the Game" was about my love affair, and "Running Scared" by Roy Orbison described what I hoped would happen. He would come back to me.

My junior year, I realized one of my fondest hopes: I joined the drill team. In white sleeveless blouses, short white starched skirts and white underpants and white boots, later to become famous as go-go boots, we twirled purple and gold nylon flags and marched beside the band. We performed during halftime at ball games and flirted with the players. I felt, briefly, like one of the pretty girls but, inside, I knew I was not—my knees knocked, my nose filled my face, my hair was never quite right.

Everyone's hair was long, including mine. We used rubber spools to curl a narrow furl along the edges, a kind of reverse page boy, and later wire curlers with brushes inside to fluff up the hair. Sleeping on either was well-nigh impossible, although the brushes were worse. Makeup—blue eye shadow, mascara, lipstick, rouge, even foundation—filled our purses and bathroom shelves. We wore stockings and garter belts to formal affairs under our prom dresses—yards and yards of netting and petticoats. For sports functions, we wore wool plaid pants and sweaters, and we dressed in costume for band and chorus and drill team extravaganzas. Life was homework, records, classes, fast cars, hamburgers and sodas, class plays, football and basketball games, piano practice, and boys, not necessarily in that order.

Although my heart was broken, I kept up my studies and performed well in school. Mrs. Gibson, my English teacher, stirred my longing to write and spurred my interest in reading. As it was, I read two to four books a week. The worlds I found in books gathered me in—anything by Zane Grey, Frank Butler, somebody Shellabarger. I loved action, adventure, romance, devouring *War and Peace, Gone with the Wind, Peyton Place.*

Mrs. Fee, my Latin and Spanish teacher, held me up as an example to everyone in her class, complimenting my Latin notebook. Little did she know that most of the boys in the class copied from my notebook. I made friends with other boys, stayed involved in school clubs, including the Ski Club and the Commercial Club, and was asked to join Quill and Pen and the Honor Society. I competed to get the best grades in all my classes, including geometry, a subject I never did understand. I even dated from time to time, managing to attend all the major dances and events with old friends.

And then it happened. Tom asked me out again. In short order, we were "going steady." Because he was no longer in school, my parents disapproved even more, but not too much was said about him specifically. I think my pining wore them down. My father and I continued to battle, but then world events finally impinged on our town and my teenage concerns.

19
We Will Bury You

During the late 1950s and into the '60s, the Cold War between the United States and the Soviet Union continued. The presence of minerals in the mountains around us and in the ground beneath our feet convinced townspeople that Kellogg was vital to any defense of America's freedoms. I suppose our isolation from the wider world gave all of us a greater sense of importance and destiny than we warranted.

The threat of nuclear war was ever present in the American mindset during this period, and headlines about the Cold War shouted from the front page of our newspaper:

SOVIETS FEAR U.S. AIR POWER, GENERAL SAYS
Has Kept Russia from Attacking America
ALL OF U.S. IN REACH OF RUSSIAN ROCKET RANGE
Reds Claim Big Missile Went over 7000 Miles
U.S. SAYS IT WILL UPHOLD DEFENSE OF ALLIES
Reply to Red Threat to Hit Plane Bases

We practiced the drill of ducking under our desks in case of attack, being sure to keep our mouths open so that our eardrums wouldn't be burst by the concussion of bombs. Bomb shelters were discussed around our dinner table, and the yellow and black three-diamond

167

sign began to appear to denote places that would serve as shelter when, not if, the Russians attacked.

Anti-Communism became an obsession in our town. The primary movers of the anti-Communist group were doctors, lawyers, businesspeople, teachers (including Mr. Exum and Mrs. Fee, and Miss George, our civics teacher), doctors' wives, and church people, the latter because Communism meant the end of religion. A student organization, I Am An American Youth Group, formed, in part with the assistance of these teachers, who acted as informal advisors. We met and heard speakers, read tracts, and debated, feeling important and informed and part of a larger movement with its foundations in patriotism.

We believed it was the personal plot of Khrushchev and the Soviets to close down *our* lead and zinc mine and smelting operations in order to weaken our country. We believed the union at the Bunker Hill, the International Mine Mill and Smelter Workers Union (Mine Mill), was infiltrated with Communists.

The seeds of this belief related back to the Communist witch-hunt in the early '50s, when my classmates and I were children. The CIO expelled the Mine Mill Union in 1950 for Communist influences. Its leadership had signed the loyalty affidavits required then by law of union officials. Those same leaders were later convicted of signing false affidavits and were appealing the convictions at a time of labor difficulties in our town. Many people in Kellogg began to feel a threat from the Mine Mill Union, resuscitating fears of Bolshevik and socialist influences lying dormant for many years, but relating back to the Western Federation of Miners and the labor wars at the turn of the twentieth century.

* * *

In cold winters, we skated on a slough at the other side of the tailings ponds between Smelterville and Pinehurst. Often the extreme temperatures extended for only a week or two, time for ice to form and, for a short period, to dig out skates—time to arrange a party, shovel snow off the ice, and build bonfires. We never lacked for wood that burned almost as soon as we touched a match to it. Under the snow in the area where we parked and built fires lay red, sandy soil or clay. Our skating rink was partially composed of seepage from the "impounded" tailings ponds. Cattails and bulrushes grew around the edges and sometimes formed small islands that we used as obstacles and cover, along with giant blackened tree stumps and whitened logs, in our games of hide and seek and crack the whip and chase the boys/girls.

Bundled against the cold, we skated and returned at intervals to our fire for warmth. In the dark fringes beyond the fire, boys passed around a bottle in a paper bag or drank beer. We were far from the lights of the mine, but a million stars flashed in the sky. Cheeks glowed, and eyes reflected the flames.

One night, high spirits erupted into a fist fight between the son of an Irish miner and the son of an Italian miner.

"Fight! Fight!"

The cry cut through the merriment. By the second shout, skaters rushed off the ice and surrounded a hump of thrashing arms and legs. In the firelight, we finally saw that they belonged to Sean and Tony.

"Oh, god, it's Tony and Sean. Sean can't fight!"

"Are they drunk? What happened?"

Both boys' hats had fallen off. Their gloves were scattered on the ground. A jacket ripped. Blood trickled down Tony's chin. Sean's face was slimy with snot and tears. The two flailed and grappled and rolled in the red clay. They churned the ground where heat had melted frost and snow. A ragged circle, including my girlfriends and I, shifted around the fight. Cheers and jeers egged the boys on. One bruised fist slammed a gory cheek. Sobs and grunts punctuated their scuffling across the ground. I walked away, then back, not wanting to see, but not wanting to miss anything either.

Tony rolled on top, pounding his fist into the side of Sean's head with a flat splat. "Take it back! Don't call me a scab, you fucker!"

Like wolves with glittering eyes, we waited for the outcome. The boys rolled again and finally separated. Sean lay struggling for breath, his body retching, his face contorted. Tony looked around, dazed. "Ah, fuck." He climbed to his knees, then his feet, picked up a jacket and smeared his bleeding nose with it. He edged over to get into his car and rested his head against the steering wheel for a minute, then turned on the engine, slammed his door, rapped his pipes, and squirreled away. The rear tires threw snow and red sand into the silent crowd.

This was our first taste of strike fever and how it would split the town.

*   *   *

During my high school years, my classmates and I were devoted to anti-Communism, to fighting the threat that our newspapers told us was incipient, that our parents said was imminent, and that our teachers warned would take away our freedom. "Better dead than red" became our slogan. We, each one of us, had to fight this creeping menace.

Khrushchev said, "We will bury you." We believed him.

Senator McCarthy and the House Un-American Activities Committee had already been discredited and the terrible blacklisting had ended years before. But in Kellogg, in the fall of 1959 and the winter, spring, summer, and fall of 1960, fear of Communism and the Russians grew almost to a fever pitch. One of the reasons was an active group of adults who fed the flames, themselves believing the end of the world as we knew it was near. My parents weren't directly involved in this group, but they were sympathizers. My mother said I couldn't read *On the Beach* by Nevil Shute, describing a world destroyed by nuclear devices, because this was part of the Communist plot—to make us lose hope in our way of life and succumb to *them*. I read it anyway.

Another reason for concern, which became increasingly clear as the year 1960 approached, was the renewal of the labor contract between Bunker Hill and the Mine Mill Union, the bargaining agent representing all of the miners. Our parents, teachers, and local newspaper pointed out that "everybody" knew the union leaders were Communists and they had perjured themselves in affidavits, just as Alger Hiss had done. Authorities on Communism came to Kellogg to speak, expounding on the dangers. A man who was a "Communist for the FBI"[6] spoke at a school assembly and to a large audience of adults in the gymnasium. From late fall into winter, management and labor bargained in an atmosphere of fear and steadily increasing antipathy in the town. They failed to renegotiate the lapsed contract.

White-collar members of the community weren't the only foes of Communism. Stories from our parents emphasized the long tradition of anti-Communism even by the workers. Jessie Rinaldi told how her husband, LaVern, joined the union in the 1930s. "The first meeting he went to, they were all Communists, and if there was anything LaVern hates, it's Communism. So, he quit the union. Before he quit, the Bunker Hill was going to fire all of those people because they all joined the union against the company."

Chuck Biotti, the miner and policeman, had his opinions, too. "You see, a union is all right, if it's run right. One night, Mine Mill called a meeting. It was supposed to be just for members and their wives. We went down and some of the top Communist leaders in Kellogg—businessmen—they were there.

"The hall was packed. These Communists had no business being there because they weren't members of the union. Pete P. was president. So I got up. I interrupted the speaker and said, 'Just a minute. Before we go any further with this meeting, I want to know: Is this a Mine Mill meeting or is it a Communist meeting?'

"Old Pete told me, 'Sit down, you're out of order.'

"I said, 'I'm not out of order. I'm not going to sit down unless you want to come down here and put me down.' Everybody gave me a big hand. I stepped right up on my feet and I told 'em, 'Let's get the rest of these Communists who don't belong here.' Old Pete rapped on the table with his gavel and said, 'Meeting adjourned.' Everybody got up and went home. That was the end of the meeting."

As the threat of a strike grew, tempers flared around town, between students, between adults, between labor and management. Getting a Communist union out of our town became a first priority for our youth group. In April 1960, the union struck, closing down all the operations except limited maintenance of the stacks to keep them from collapsing and the pumps to keep water out of the underground drifts.

By May, our I Am An American Youth Group planned a parade and rally, a "demonstration" in later 1960s terminology, to show the union up as Communist. We called it a demonstration of patriotism, a demonstration against Communism in all its forms. We were incensed when union leaders accused us of "union-breaking." Our response was some version of "If the shoe fit," but our private conversations all had to do with getting rid of the Communistic Mine Mill union. Warnings came from the union, both locally and nationally, that the students would open a boil and be hurt themselves if they proceeded. The local anti-Communist group sprang to our defense. A sampling of the newspaper headlines reflected the tug of war over the students and the parade:

KELLOGG YOUTH MOVEMENT GAINS BIG APPROVAL
Business Firms Back Americanism Parade
American Legion Backs Anti-Communist Drive
Strike Issues Outlined by Union; Company

Through a large advertisement in the *Kellogg Evening News*, we invited everyone to our event:

PUBLIC INVITATION
We Especially Invite Citizens of Shoshone County to Witness
our parade and Americanism Rally
Thursday, May 26, in Kellogg at 5:00 P.M.
"I Am An American Youth Movement"

Who paid for that ad? As far as I know, we didn't. And then more headlines:

Local Youth Movement Gains Further Support
YOUTH MOVEMENT PARADE RALLY SET FOR TONIGHT
Huge Crowds Attend Youth Parade-Rally

Union members would attack the students, we heard. Be prepared for a "rumble." Volunteer band members—a majority of the band—marched down Main and McKinley to the ballpark. Men teachers walked alongside to protect the players from harm. I was no longer in the band but marched with the other students, feeling patriotic and brave, fighting Communism with my friends. The events passed without mishap, serving only to increase the rancor in town and set students against their parents who belonged to or supported the Mine Mill union.

Many miners believed Bunker Hill was behind the whole youth movement. Union members knew the history of the labor wars in northern Idaho; most of us did not. No one from Bunker Hill participated directly in our planning or parade. The fathers of several leaders worked for Bunker in mid-management positions, but the fathers of others belonged to the union.

Reporters from *Time* magazine were in town. They wrote about Kellogg, calling the town dreary and pointing out that the mountains were so high and close around the town that the sun shone only a few hours each day, as if this were a character defect. The article said people lived in shanties warmed by single oil burners and ate beans and 'dogs as a regular diet. The high school students who paraded down the main street carrying signs that read "Better Dead than Red" were brainwashed by the anti-Communists, and the mining company was saving money in a down market while miners starved.

It was hard to believe the *Time* reporters hadn't seen what I knew was true: my town was rich with friendly people, successful businesses, a basketball team that went to State four out of the last five years, and well-paid miners at five or six dollars an hour or better, compared to a minimum wage of one dollar. Unlike other small towns, we had culture: school band and chorus extravaganzas every year, musical plays produced by students, and community concerts with traveling artists every three or four months.

After the parade and rally at the football field and the brief national attention, summer settled in and emotions quieted down for a month or two. Thick black headlines ceased appearing in the newspaper. The strike continued. Bunker Hill had little motivation to negotiate: lead and zinc prices were at an all-time low. Many men left town to get work elsewhere, leaving their families at home with the assurance that when the strike ended, they would return.

* * *

Every summer, three high school girls from Kellogg went to Girls' State in Boise, meeting other girls from towns all around the state. These activities were sponsored by the American Legion with the intention of teaching young people about state government and their civic responsibilities. In the summer of 1960, I was selected to go, along with two friends, Sylvia and Karen.

In accordance with a years-old format, we convened into a legislature with committees, proposed and enacted "laws," and elected a governor, lieutenant governor, and speaker from among our members. Each of us was to give a speech and perform some talent —piano playing, singing, dramatic reading—not unlike a small Miss America pageant, although beauty wasn't supposed to be part of this playacting.

We held our legislative sessions, studied and adopted a constitution. We girls from north Idaho insisted on including a "Bill of Obligations," having to do with loyalty. I shudder when I read some of the sections now. In addition to requiring everyone to vote, get an eighth-grade education, learn what Communism is and how to fight it, receive training in Civil Defense, establish bomb shelters in towns of more than three thousand, and perform public service, the Bill requires "each citizen who is a teacher or holds a public office to sign a non-Communist affidavit upon penalty of fine or imprisonment or both." The federal government is "obligated to and must enforce" all such requirements.

We were children when McCarthy and the witch-hunters were in full cry over loyalty oaths, and yet, we had fallen into the same mode of thinking, assisted by the anti-Communist group in Kellogg, who seemed to be enjoying their own hysteria. Their solution, as was McCarthy's, was less freedom and more regulation for supposed safety. They, and we, weren't willing to trust to the First Amendment rights of free speech and freedom of association or to the workings of democracy to keep our town, state, and country free.

Late summer of 1960 in Kellogg was hot. The strike fund was gradually being depleted. Nightly charges and counter-charges appeared again in the headlines of the *Kellogg Evening News*. The plight of miners' families grew increasingly difficult, as union reserves for food and rent were disappearing, and many men had left town. My friend Betty's father was in Alaska; Diane's father drove daily to Coeur d'Alene to work odd jobs. Whole families left and our town seemed to be dwindling away. Betty was afraid her family would leave; I arranged with my mother to have Betty live with us if they did move.

It was a difficult summer for other reasons, too. My father continued to disapprove of my "true love." He forbade me to see him, and the battle was joined. He threatened; I rebelled. Finally, my mother called Bob Robson, my father's lawyer friend, asking for his help in the war between my father and me. Bob hired me to work for him the rest of the summer and then after school and on Saturdays and during vacations in my senior year, thereby reducing the amount of time my father and I were together.

* * *

When I think back on that time of obsession, for me and for the town, I am somewhat at a loss to understand it, but ultimately it had far-reaching consequences. I, like most of my friends, had no clear knowledge of the forces that drove all adolescents—hormones, peers, insecurities. By and large, we were all good girls. Most of us attended church, worked hard at school, helped raise money for charities, took ourselves seriously as the up-and-coming generation charged with protecting our country against Communism. Some of my friends drank beer; some smoked. I did not and because I was an A student and probably a "square" (our term for straight-arrows or geeks), I couldn't understand why my parents didn't trust me to make decisions about my own life.

Later I understood some of their reasons. During that summer of 1960, I kept up a steady correspondence with a friend who was out of town. My mother saved all of my friend's letters to me. They reflected that one, and then another, and then another, of my friends and acquaintances married. All the brides were pregnant and young—one a soon-to-be junior, several soon-to-be seniors, two just out of high school. An acquaintance left town to have a baby. Abortion, of course, was not an alternative, and even if it had been, I doubt it would have stopped the weddings, all with white dresses, bridesmaids, showers. My mother was appalled. I thought it was romantic.

Every aspect of our lives seemed to be black or white during this time. If you weren't an anti-Communist, you must be a Communist. In the developing debates between Richard Nixon and John Kennedy in the run for president, if you were for Medicare, then you were in favor of socialized medicine; if for federal funding of schools, then you wanted government control. If you favored Nixon, you were anti-Roman Catholic. If you believed in a miners' union, you must be at least a socialist. The same black-white views often spilled over into our personal lives. We were friends, or we were enemies. If a girl was pregnant, she married. We loved our parents, or we hated them.

20
We're All Hanging Here

Tall, blond, with a cackling laugh, a prominent nose, and a compassionate heart, Bob Robson took as clients anyone who needed help, whether they could pay or not. His father, a former executive assistant for the general manager of Bunker Hill, served as his collection agent, but quit when Bob wouldn't let him try to get money from anyone who might have a hard time paying. Bob's wife, Penny, a southern belle and a whiz at mathematics whom he'd met while in the service, raised their four blond children and belonged to all the ladies' clubs with my mother. They lived in a small house next to the Bunker Hill office building, a sublease from Bob's parents.

The Robson Law Office was a small storefront next to Hutton's Department Store at the town end of McKinley Avenue. A large metal desk and four chairs filled a small reception area. If four clients sat down at once, their knees would almost touch. Bob's office was through an inside door. A coffee machine and duplicating equipment sat in the hallway between the entry and his office. Old-style venetian blinds covered the store window, and we kept them drawn so people couldn't look in and see who was waiting to talk with an attorney.

On my first day of work, Bob sat me down in his office, but to do so, we had to clear a chair of books and papers. Bookshelves topped with more stacks and files lined the walls, and framed diplomas from the University of Idaho on the back wall outlined his head. He explained the kind of work he did, which was a little bit of everything—divorces, wills, lawsuits for personal injuries and contract disputes, real estate purchases and sales, along with a boundary dispute or two ("the worst kind of fight between neighbors who ought to get along," he said), even some criminal work because he acted as prosecuting attorney for the town. Everything but collection work. "I won't be a squeeze-blood," he said. He emphasized the importance of confidentiality in everything he did, and as a secretary, I would be an extension of him. His solemnity on this subject impressed me. I felt I was being entrusted with adult responsibilities, and I was.

Shari, Bob's full-time secretary, set me up next to her at a small table with a manual typewriter, a store of letterhead stationery, envelopes, and legal-sized paper. She sat behind the big reception desk with her electric typewriter, files, stacked shelves for paper and envelopes, a large ledger, and office supplies.

My first few days, I typed letters, bills, more letters, more bills, and read legal descriptions of land to Shari. I wasn't certain I was really needed. Clients came in and spoke to her. Bob gave her important papers to type, asked how I was doing, told us a joke or two. But before long, they gave me legal briefs and wills to type.

After Shari left every day at 5:00, I usually worked on, often into the dinner hour. Bob worked too. Sometimes I stayed past his leave-taking. Often, he called me into his office and explained what he was doing with one client or another, referring to law books and briefs. Other evenings, he gossiped with me—not about his clients but about the town. He would lean back in his chair, prop his foot on his desk, and launch into a story, like the one about The Lighthouse.

*   *   *

The law office began to feel like home, and I looked forward every day to going to work. I was good at typing letters and legal documents. I even liked to file, to Shari's delight, and staple the heavy blue backing paper on wills. Answering the telephone and talking to clients who came in the door made me feel important and needed. When Shari was there, I sat at the small typewriter table, facing the venetian blinds. It was a cramped space, but I managed. When she left for the day and on Saturday mornings, I sat behind the big metal desk and used the electric typewriter, pretending the job was all mine.

I sent out bills, straightened the desk, replenished the paper stocks—Robert M. Robson letterhead, second pages, carbon paper, numbered legal-sized court paper, will paper, envelopes, and onion skin. Just the feel of the will paper, cream white and thick, and the will backs, powder blue and stiff, made these documents special. So did the ritual surrounding them. After we typed a will, with *no* mistakes, and enclosed them in blue backing, the client came in to sign. I wasn't old enough to serve as a witness, but I rounded up two people from the insurance office next door. The three witnesses (including Shari) and the client listened as Bob explained that they were being asked to certify that the document was being signed by the client and that the client was in sound mind and understood what he or she was signing. Everyone knew each other, so this request was not made of strangers. The pens scratched and few words were spoken. When the witnesses left, Bob shook his client's hand, and then he laughed.

We used carbon paper to make copies of all letters and documents. Wills were the most difficult—five or six copies with carbon paper between each foolscap sheet. Typed letters on the last copy or two were barely visible. For some purposes, we used a duplicating machine or stencil. The machine paper felt wet and slick and I didn't like to touch it. When we needed lots of copies, we typed a stencil master on a brilliant blue waxlike surface. The typewriter keys cut the letters and numbers through the wax. Then we attached the stencil sheet, handling it very carefully so it wouldn't tear or the *o*'s fall out, and attached it to a cylinder from which ink was dispensed through the stencil onto white paper. We cranked the cylinder and page after page slid through from one end, coming out the other as copies. *Voila!* It could make tens of copies, but eventually the stencil gave out.

My responsibilities grew. I made appointments for people who called or poked their heads in the door, asking if Bob was there. I drafted simple letters, and explained procedures to clients. I was no longer a charity case who needed a home away from home. The points of contact with my father, around the dinner table primarily, dwindled to almost nothing. Bob's plan was working.

Often he talked about my father, admiring his skills as a doctor, explaining his flaws—gambling and drinking—and suggesting some of the demons that drove him: fear of failures in his doctoring and as a father and husband, fear of not being good enough for my mother. Bob was the first and only person to discuss my father's drinking with me, or even to mention it out loud, and he told me, in one of those evening sessions, that he wanted me to work for him because he thought I needed time away from my father. At first, I was offended that it wasn't my qualities that had prompted him to offer me my job. He pricked that balloon in his honest way and reassured me, whinnying his laugh. Shari, he said, needed time to collect money from clients. He needed me to do the secretarial work.

Bob talked about the strike too, and I learned more from him than from the newspapers. Over 1,600 men were on strike. Bunker had a total of 2,400 salaried and wage earners with a payroll of one million dollars a month. The prices of metal were low: nine cents a pound for lead and eleven cents for zinc. Silver was twenty-one cents an ounce. He said the Bunker's break-even point was eleven cents on lead and thirteen cents on zinc. After the student parade, Bob helped organize the Common Sense Council along with Glenn Exum and others because, he said, "It wasn't right that a bunch of kids were confronting these hardheads." He wrote essays damning both sides and read them on the radio. "Get together and settle this strike," he importuned. "We're all hanging here."

The strike wore on. People wore down. The union and company representatives had even ceased meeting to negotiate their differences. The fear that the mines would never reopen began to surface and rancor grew stronger against the Mine Mill union. It was in this uneasy setting and after one of Bob's radio essays that several miners came to him for help in ending the impasse. I was excited. Here was an opportunity to take part in something that we as students could only dream about in our Americanism group.

Bob had always been fairly philosophical about the union and its alleged ties to Communism. He, like the other businesses, wanted the strike to end and thought the Mine Mill union demand for an increase of 22½ cents per hour was unreasonable. He also believed that the company's responses, particularly the refusal to talk for a three-month period in the summer, were high-handed, a minority opinion among the white-collar crowd. Bob and the cadre of miners who came to see him offered Kellogg a solution different than anyone had contemplated: kick the Mine Mill union out as a bargaining agent for the miners.

The men came in and out of the office. Bob, not previously a labor lawyer, bought a labor manual and casebooks and studied the problem. He explained some of the questions and possible solutions to me, often just thinking out loud. What he and the men planned was a decertification election. He warned the men that the union was watching his office and fretted sometimes about my working late, but didn't make me stop. To keep a low profile, some meetings were held in the beauty shop of one of the miner's wives.

To oust an existing union, it would be necessary to gather support from the current members for the election. Getting enough signatures was a huge undertaking, often fraught with overtones of danger or violence. Even getting the list of members took skullduggery: "One of the people helping me knew a janitor at the clinic," Bob said. "He snuck a list off the office manager's desk [all the union members had health coverage] and photocopied and gave it to me."

Before long, the men realized if the Mine Mill union were ousted, there would be *no* union, a situation they couldn't abide. They were ready to quit their effort. Bob studied and worked, then proposed a solution: form a new union to get bargaining rights for all miners. All it took was two or three men associating together, and this they did, naming their new union the Northwest Metalworkers Union, which was immediately labeled a "company" union by the Mine Mill union, one organized by Bunker Hill to challenge the existing, or "workers" union. Bob called the men behind the new union movement the Fearsome Five because, he said, "They were willing to stick their necks out and take the heat. The Mine Mill was putting out food and groceries and making payments on cars until it went broke. The damned governor of the state gave the strikers state aid. That really pissed me off. I went to Boise and told him off."

The new union ran out of money to pay Bob's bills, the filing fees, and the costs of soliciting signatures. All seemed lost. When Bob called a meeting to say that he had received an anonymous contribution, the men questioned him. They would never accept funds from Bunker Hill; they were longtime employees, most of them, and as leery of the company as the old union members were. He assured them the money didn't come from the mining company, and they accepted his word. The new union was back in business. Years later, Bob explained to me that the money came from the anti-Communist group, but they in turn received it from a third party—not Bunker, he swore.

All fall, we—and I use this term royally—filled in applications to the National Labor Relations Board, gathered men's signatures, plotted and planned. Bob and his family moved from their house, which was owned by Bunker, to Sunnyside. The general manager of Bunker Hill told all his management that they couldn't even talk to Bob *or* his wife. Since my mother wasn't connected with the Bunker, we saw quite a bit of Penny and Bob. They played bridge with my parents and the four of them went out to dinner. Otherwise, Penny was isolated from many of her longtime friends among the wives of Bunker management.

Any miner connected with the new union was a pariah in town and cut off from Mine Mill benefits. One of the Fearsome Five was thrown out of the Mine Mill union because his car was seen outside Bob's office. He went back over to the union hall with a gun and ended up in jail. Bob, as city attorney, had to prosecute him, but persuaded him to plead guilty, pay a fine, and got him out. Some of the former Mine Mill members were having difficulty even buying groceries. Bob arranged for several doctors' wives to collect food. In addition, he found some willing souls, or, as he called them, "a couple of characters to poach deer for us." Bob and "his team" were feeding almost sixty families before the strike ended.

An election campaign needed a savvy manager. With part of the anonymous money, Bob hired a campaign manager who came to town to design a newspaper and radio campaign. He stayed in Wallace because he was afraid of the Mine Mill members. Whenever Bob visited the motel room to pick up copy, he was greeted by the manager holding a crow bar as protection. One of the full-page newspaper ads showed a woman standing in front of an empty lunch pail and a little boy beside her. The words under the picture were: "I wonder if I'll ever pack this lunch bucket again." Bob persuaded the local radio station to play "White Christmas" every hour on the hour. We kept getting calls from his friends, asking "When are you going to stop that *tinkle tinkle tinkle*?"

In the end, an election was held but not without several slips and wrong turns in both the business and legal processes. And in the end, the new union won out, by a "cat's whisker" as Bob said, twenty-one votes. The strike ended just before Christmas of my senior year.

Chuck Biotti was present as a policeman at the Mine Mill union hall shortly after the election results were announced. He described what happened: "When the union went out on the long strike in 1960, I was on the police force. The Mine Mill thought they had the election won. They had a great big celebration planned down at the hall. There was a table all laden with food. The results of the election came in that the Mine Mill lost the election—that was one time they had a secret ballot. All that food—meat, vegetables, and salads—they just went over and picked up the containers of food and scattered it all over the hall like a bunch of pigs. You should have seen the main floor out there. Oh, man, it was six inches deep with slop. Then the Northwest Metal union took over."

When our side won the union election, I celebrated with the miners. We, Bob and I and the workers, had done it. Bob went in to negotiate the new contract. He said, "I told the president we'll have to take what you give us, but you better be damn careful. I'm a fast learner, and if you screw me this time, I'm gonna get you the next time." Bob got a good contract, including a one-hundred-dollar advance for Christmas for each union member.

I felt I had been in the middle of an exciting Zane Grey western, helping to face down the forces of evil, something like a shoot-out on Main Street.

21

He Couldn't Breathe

The incandescent light bulb burned hot. In the closet where it stayed lit from one shift to the next, rags dirty with oil lay heaped on the top shelf above supplies—nails, bolts, chains, grease, oil cans, fuse lengths. One tendril of smoke drifted from a rag, then another, then a flame licking at cloth and the creosoted wood door-jamb. When the fumes combusted, the door exploded open and fire and smoke ripped outward, fed by volatile compounds in the timbers lining the mined-out drifts and hazardous fumes. James, my guide in the Bunker Hill mine, speculated this was how the Sunshine Mine fire began on May 2, 1972.

On the surface, such a fire could be contained quickly. But 3,400 feet underground in the country's richest and deepest silver mine, the Sunshine, the fire could burn unnoticed for long, precious minutes, even hours. Unnoticed, that is, until the smoke filled the drifts and traveled along the tunnels to the shafts where the hoists carry men down to work and the ore out for processing.

Dark, toxic clouds of smoke filled the hoist area of the No. 10 Chippy, the main lift. Miners, 173 of them, worked above and below the 3,400-foot level, some more than a mile deep. Smoke dropped down the No. 10 shaft and spread outward, obscuring the hoist shack, filling the tunnels leading to the shaft.

Men continued to work at 3,700 feet, 4,600 feet, 4,800 feet,

5,600 feet. When someone at last smelled smoke and sounded the alarm, they headed for the hoist to be taken up. Over fifty men reached a level where they could walk out just minutes ahead of the descending cloud. Thirty men crammed into a skip and headed up from the 4,400-foot level. The thirty-first man couldn't get on. The miners in the skip died of smoke inhalation at the 3,700-foot level, and the man who missed the skip walked out alive. The hoistman on the Chippy died, and no one else could get out. By then, ninety-three men remained trapped underground.

For eight days, Sunshine mounted rescue efforts. Family and friends camped outside the mine, waiting for news, fearful of the bad, praying for the good. My father and the other doctors descended to the upper levels, hoping injured men would be found and brought to them. A rescue crew descended the Silver Summit shaft, approximately three-quarters of a mile from the No. 10 shaft, to the 3,000-foot level and made their way toward the Chippy. Smoke forced them back. Another crew descended the Jewel Shaft where most of the survivors had come out, three-quarters of a mile in the opposite direction from the No. 10 shaft, and then took the No. 12 shaft to the 4,800-foot level.

The rescuers finally found two men still alive at the 4,800-foot level, not far from where seven other men didn't make it. Tom Wilkinson and Ron Flory survived because they were far enough from the smoke to avoid inhalation and because they'd brought their lunches to work on May 2, and eaten the lunches of several of the dead men. The other ninety-one miners perished, some in the skip, others in smoke-filled tunnels.

The Sunshine fire disaster was the worst ever in the Coeur d'Alene mining area. It was after this fire that the self-rescue units became mandatory equipment for all miners.

A larger-than-life statue of a miner holding a jackdrill stands as a memorial just off the freeway at the turnoff to the Sunshine Mine up Big Creek. The miner's lamp on his hardhat lights the night, every night. Below the statue, a plaque names the miners who died. Although the fire occurred over a decade after I left home, many of the names are familiar—boys I knew in high school and fathers of boys and girls who attended school with me. One casualty was the son of my Spanish and Latin teacher, Mrs. Fee.

*   *   *

Perhaps all students have a Mrs. Fee in their school memories. A combination of tender heart, nerves highly strung, affection for students, love of her subjects, and high expectations created a less than effective teacher. Anyone missing assignments or flunking could get around her with a sad story: made-up dead grandmothers or great aunts, hangovers disguised as blinding headaches, dog-eats-homework tales. Tapping pencils (four or five in unison) caused her to draw her shoulders together, narrow her eyes, and shake all over. My friend took out his glass eye once and sent her raving from the classroom. And yet, most of us learned some Spanish, some Latin. What Mrs. Fee liked best to talk about, and what we listened to best, were her stories of bull fights and bullfighters. Whether she really experienced all she recounted to us, we never knew. But few reunions end without some reminiscing about Mrs. Fee.[7]

I visited her in the summer of 1994 in Wallace, where she lived.

When she answered the door, a clear tube extended from her nose down her chest and between her legs. A trail of tubing led back through the room behind her, and beyond. Thin hair, darker on the ends and white around her part, hung in drooping ringlets on either side of her face. Only her strong teeth in a wide grimace, and her dark eyes bright with manic excitement behind her glasses, were recognizable in the bony structure of her head.

"Mrs. Fee! How are you?"

"Not well. You know. Not well." Her skeleton hand grabbed my arm. "So good of you to come. You are so beautiful." She held the screen door open with her slippered foot, and beckoned. "Come into my parlor." Her eyes glinted. When she was sure I was inside the door, she turned and walked slowly into the living room.

Along one wall, books towered over us. An oil painting of a man—he could have been a banker so gray was he—hung in one corner so that its image was reflected in the mirror on the second wall. A crimson aura around his head shocked my eye. Photographs, colored glass birds with long pointed beaks, propped-up postcards, black lacquered boxes inlaid with mother of pearl, a crystal prism reflecting rainbow patterns, a miniature sculptured miner with a drill, a ceramic vase with two dead yellow roses, and a pack of Carlton cigarettes crowded together on an elaborately carved sideboard. Magazines and books were strewn across the matching coffee table. Two padded chairs, one covered with Naugahyde, the other a faded floral print material, faced the davenport.

"Sit down, my dear. Sit down. It is so good of you to come." The plastic tubing curled around the floor behind Mrs. Fee and led to a machine shaped much like a stereo speaker with a bellows front. Warm stuffy air filled the room from shoulder level up. When I dropped into the Naugahyde chair, I felt the difference in the temperature. It was almost comfortable. Mrs. Fee lowered herself carefully into the floral chair. Beside it stood a TV tray littered with papers, books, and magazines and a red, white, and blue Federal Express envelope on top. In front of her chair was a small footstool with no room for feet.

"It's my hip. You know. Ever since I broke it, it has hurt me." Her hand crept along the side of her leg, no bigger round than my wrist. "Here. Feel that." She stood again, grabbed my hand and guided it to her hip bone. Through her denim pants, I felt an indentation on the side of her leg. "It did not heal properly." She sat and slipped forward on the chair and leaned her elbows on her knees. "Do you know how I broke it?"

I asked her if she fell.

"You see those books?" She motioned to the shelves. Every row was crammed full. Books about lost cities, forgotten civilizations. Religious tomes; pamphlets on UFOs. A Time-Life series on *Mysteries of the Unknown*. Shakespeare, Hugo, Ludlum. A Judith Krantz lay open on her side table. On top of the books on the highest shelf, others were stacked in a precarious ladder reaching almost to the ceiling—*Dictionary of Phrase and Fable, Masterpieces of World Philosophy in Summary Form*, art books, tracts on the world religions, Sidney Sheldon novels, and *The Collected Works of William Faulkner*. "They fell. On me." She laughed wheezily and her eyes glowed. "Maybe they will again."

"Could I take those on top and stack them someplace else?"

"Oh, no. My basement is full of books. There is no place else to put them."

Through the living room door, past the coiled tubing, I saw a dining table covered with papers, and to the right, a bedroom. A corner of the bed told the same tale: books, papers, boxes, clothes, pictures. If Mrs. Fee slept there, she shared the space with a closet's worth of objects.

Two additional paintings hung on the walls, one of a young man with black-framed glasses, another of a girl with Titian hair whom I recognized as a younger, vibrant Mrs. Fee with rosy cheeks, eager eyes, upswept hair just beginning to turn gray. On all the portraits but hers, the name E. Fee was scribbled along the lower edge.

"My father was an Englishman. He went to Oxford. It was the frontier that pulled him to Montana." She followed my gaze to the portrait in the mirror. "My friend Maude won't visit until I change the red. A devil's aura. So silly. Don't you think it sets Dex off just fine?"

I nodded.

"Dex was my husband. You knew him, didn't you?"

I said not.

"He died several years before Norman did." She thought a moment. "I can't remember when that was." She plucked a tissue from the box on the stool in front of her. "Poor Norman. He worked so hard and took such good care of me. He was a good son. He died in the mining disaster. You know." Mrs. Fee stood and walked to the other room. I followed. We stood before the man-with-glasses painting. "Norman was very handsome, don't you think?"

The pale face with black-rimmed glasses and dark hair seemed a younger version of the bankerlike father in the living room painting. Next to the pink eagerness of his mother's portrait, Norman was a pale shadow.

"Fire underground swallowed all the oxygen. When the hoistman died, the rest were stranded. A mile below sea level. No one wore the self-rescue units. They were stored someplace else. The men suffocated. No air. Norman couldn't breathe." Her eyes emptied and turned flat. I looked again at the small sculpture of the miner on the coffee table. It was a replica of the memorial along the road, but this one had glasses, tiny and black like those one saw on small gold elephants when Barry Goldwater ran for president in 1964.

Mrs. Fee died not long after I visited her.

* * *

Accidents happened frequently in the mines: broken bones, severed toes and fingers, gashes, scrapes, cuts and bruises. Cave-ins buried men; rock bursts killed them. Before the Sunshine Mine disaster, the accidents were usually limited to one or two or three men at a time. Most recovered and returned to the mining work. Some, like Gordie Parker, were disabled for life. Even men who escaped the disaster in the Sunshine returned to work underground. Mining was their calling and their lives, until the mines closed.

22

How's Your Body? III

My father died in September 1978, one week before he turned sixty-two.

On a visit home, my last while he was alive, I picked out a few bars of a Mozart concerto on the piano. Dad came into the room and listened. "Play something more," he said.

"I can remember only a few lines," I said. "It's been too long."

"Don't be stupid. Get up." He sat down and played *Twelfth Street Rag*. "I learned that when I was sixteen—forty-five years ago."

"You have a better memory than I do. I don't remember anything I used to play."

He slammed down the key cover and stood up. "Goddam waste of money giving you kids all those lessons," he said and stalked from the room.

Our rowls went up and down over the years, but eventually we reached an uneasy peace. From Seattle, I called him at work and we had long friendly conversations. I believe he finally respected my accomplishments, and perhaps my being a lawyer helped, too. I worked in a man's world. His generosity financed college, law school, and a car. From a distance, he provided moral support, encouraging me always to seek more responsibility and independence. Good news and I called him. See what a good girl am I.

Difficult news and the facts of my life—lovers, trysts, divorces—and I called him. Don't tell Mom. See how much like you I am.

On the night after that last visit, I stayed in Spokane, Washington, attending the Washington State Bar Association convention. The alarm rang beside me. I reached to turn it off and picked up the telephone receiver instead. "Yes." Yes, I was in a hotel room. Yes, I was sleeping and you woke me up. Yes, who's calling me?

"Julie. This is your mother. Dad is in the hospital in Coeur d'Alene. I'm in Moscow. Julie, can you go to him? I shouldn't have left."

"Yes," I said again, sitting up, swinging my legs to the floor. "Why is he at the hospital? He was all right this afternoon." "All right" was a relative term. He'd been used up, sagging and old, recovering from myocarditis (an inflammation of the sac around his heart) but had acted his usual self.

"The hired man took him. He coughed up blood. I'm leaving Moscow now. I'll meet you there in about two hours. I shouldn't have left." She hung up.

The drive at two in the morning was dark and fast, and I have no memory of the thirty miles from Spokane, Washington, to Coeur d'Alene, Idaho. Now the details return: the new, blue hospital off one of the highway exits, the walk from the front entrance along a corridor with no one else in it, my footsteps loud and hurried in my ears, to the emergency room and then to the ICU. No ether smells in this hospital, just carpet chemicals. My father lay flat on his back, legs splayed under the sheet.

I stood beside the hospital bed in the intensive care unit, talking to him while a doctor and nurse worked over him. He knew I was there, or maybe not the "I" that was his daughter Julie, but the "I" that was a part of his flesh. The nurse was my friend Betty's sister.

"My arms itch," he said, rubbing his left hand on his right forearm. Inside, his life's blood had burst a bubble in his aorta and spilled into the spaces around his heart and outside his lungs. He was a doctor. Did he know this?

"It'll be all right," I said. I rubbed his arm. "You'll be okay." His skin, freckled with age spots, moved loosely over bone and muscle. My hand held his hand, trembling, wide and without calluses, the hand that knew disease and pain and tried to cure one and dull the other. His hair was limp and gray. Only that afternoon when I had come to visit, taking a break from the Bar Convention in Spokane, it was like *his* father's—still dark with only one streak of white in it. The hollow bags under his eyes were deep enough to climb into.

The bed was too narrow to keep him safe and alive. The sheet pulled up across his bare chest was white, the walls green—why are all hospital walls green? Across the gray screen of the wall-mounted monitor, a yellow line marched, gyrating up and down, an earth-quake line, tracing the fault of my father's heart as it tried to pump oxygen to his brain, blood to his limbs, and kept breaking.

"I'm cold," my father said. He looked into my eyes. Fear and knowledge leapt from his synapses to mine.

"You'll be okay. It'll be all right." My broken record, the song I played over and over, didn't cure the aneurysm, didn't dull his fear. It was only me whistling in the dark to myself. I didn't know what to say. Cold, wrapped like a cube inside me, gripped my chest.

"Julie, you have to leave for a few minutes," the nurse said. "We need to try something else."

"No." I gripped his hand and felt him return the pressure. "No." The quake line pulsed slowly, the breaks in his earth diminishing.

"Just a few minutes." She guided me away from the bed.

I looked back at the monitor. The yellow line on the gray screen peaked once, twice, and droned a straight line. She closed the door.

*   *   *

When my mother arrived, I was alone in the room. She walked to the shell that had encased my father. "Glennie, I'm here." She picked up his hand. I watched the yellow line, a moving string with no blips.

"I came as fast as I could. I shouldn't have left you this afternoon. Glennie, I love you." She dropped into the chair beside this shell, and lowered her head to his side. "I love you." I hoped he heard her, wherever he was. He wasn't in that room anymore.

My mother has told me, "If I had left your father, I don't think he would have been as good a doctor as he was." When I think in terms of how many people he helped, how many patients he did save, I know she may be right. The two of them were an important part of Kellogg. In some ways, I think of them as emblematic of the town: so much of their surface lives seemed ordinary and happy, the way they appeared when they danced, but under the surface my father, at least, led a darker life. His drinking, gambling, and verbal outrages affected our family just as the smelter, the smoke, the lead and arsenic affected the people and land of our town.

Our family gathered before the funeral at our lake place where my parents lived. The body that was my father's lay in the mortuary in Kellogg. I did not enter that room, but I passed it and stole a glance. The profile of his face was a stone. Without his glasses, he seemed a mere mannequin. And then my mother closed the lid for the funeral.

An honor guard of nurses, each dressed in white starched cap, dress, and stockings, stood like wings on either side of the elaborate coffin at the front of the church. His doctor partners served as pallbearers, along with Jim Bening and Bob Robson, and an extra six of friends, a double ring of hands. Townspeople—miners, wives, businessmen and women, gambling and drinking buddies, Tommy's Trio, my friends, their parents, teachers, coaches, patients, not-patients—filled the church, spilled into the parking lot, sang hymns, shed tears. The Episcopal priest, Father McReynolds, who had been one of my father's gin rummy partners and was shaking with Parkinson's, eulogized him.

"How's your body?" he began. A low wave of laughter filled the church. "No one who knew Doc Whitesel would ever say he was without failings. But I like to think he earned a place in heaven in spite of those failings, common to us all, in one form or another. Glen was our doctor, our friend, and an irreplaceable man in Kellogg, Idaho." He faced the casket and added, "See you later, alligator."

23

The Fish Swallowed the Whale

I graduated from high school in May 1961, and left for Seattle, Washington, in June. By September, I was married, and in early 1962, my daughter Melanie was born. I never returned to Kellogg to live, but because my father continued to work there until 1978, I visited frequently.

The town thrived during this period and beyond. In 1968, when Bunker Hill was reporting some of the largest earnings in its history, it waged a bitter battle against takeover by Gulf Resources & Chemical, a much smaller company headquartered in Houston, Texas, that wanted to add the mine to its other mineral resource holdings. In the end, Gulf Resources won and the fish swallowed the whale, as nearly everyone in town labeled the merger. Still, hopes were high that this merger would continue the prosperity of the Coeur d'Alene Mining District. Perhaps the then-president of the company saw the future with better eyes than most. He quit, refusing to work for Gulf, a company he believed would exploit the minerals and care little for the town. He was right.

The 1960 strike, while a defining moment in my life, faded away from public consciousness, although the remnants of this war between company and workers remained simmering in the annals of union memories, to boil over again years later. The new union held the loyalty of most miners for a number of years, but finally the

United Steel Workers of America gained a toehold and ultimately won a representation election to become the primary union at Bunker Hill.

During the 1960 strike, Bunker Hill built a phosphoric acid plant. This facility was designed to take sulfuric acid from the zinc plant, mix it with phosphate rock purchased out of area, and produce phosphoric acid, a component of fertilizer. Another fertilizer facility was built in 1966–67. Nevertheless, the sulfur dioxide content in the atmosphere remained high.

Because environmental regulations for clean air were tightening, another acid plant was installed in 1970. Still, the sulfur dioxide levels in the atmosphere were higher than allowed under government rules, so the company decided to build two new chimneys to disperse the sulfur dioxide that wasn't captured in the acid plants. The taller of the two was at the lead smelter, 715 feet, and the second rose 610 feet at the zinc plant.

*　*　*

From Seattle, I returned to Kellogg for my ten-year high school reunion, dressed in lace hot pants and bearing stories of earning my law degree and pictures of Melanie, then almost ten years old. My girlfriends were all dolled up, too. The boys had taken fewer pains, but mostly they, too, seemed spruced up for the occasion. All the couples who married in high school or shortly after were still married, except me. Old flames asked me to dance and I felt more popular than I ever had while in school. We all drank and some of us smoked and talked long into the night, swapping stories of successes. Alan came with his beautiful black wife and no one batted an eyelash at her; we all tried to hide our amazement at how handsome he had grown. Another classmate, one of the few dressed in a suit, hovered around the edges of the room, almost unrecognizable. Rumors circulated that he worked for the CIA, which he would not confirm.

The Bunker was running full bore, churning out lead, silver, and zinc, and Kellogg and the surrounding towns almost glowed in the mining prosperity of the whole region. We all promised to keep in touch and many of us, after three days of strutting, gossiping, laughing, drinking and dancing, and remembering briefly the classmates who weren't there, returned to our other lives away from Kellogg.

Kellogg continued to prosper, but the effects of mining began to nag. Sulfur dioxide wasn't the only problem. Lead shavings and particulates, arsenic, and cadmium were also released during the smelting and other metal refining processes. The bag house at the smelter caught most of the lead, but in 1974 a fire destroyed hundreds of the wool bags. Gulf Resources continued smelting anyway, running the smelter without the bags for six months, depositing the equivalent of eleven years' worth of emissions into the air during that period.[8]

Almost two hundred children living in the area of the smelter were found to have elevated lead levels, and a lawsuit against Bunker (Gulf) came down with a judgment of $8.8 million for lead poisoning a few years later. Court records from this lawsuit were closed. Not too surprisingly, the people who lived in Kellogg came to the defense of Bunker, because they didn't want the Environmental Protection Agency or the Occupational Safety and Health Administration to close down the mine. My father was one of the doctors charged with testing the children and he believed the poisoning was an anomaly, as he was unaware of what Gulf had done. Few of the townspeople knew about the extremely high emissions, which only came to light years later, and were defended by a Gulf official as necessary because the lead prices were so high and therefore profitable and a fix would take too much time.[9] Mining supported the livelihood of everyone in town. Distrust of the government ran high anyway in this area of small towns and hard labor, and the EPA requirements that continued to pile onto the major employer seemed to almost everyone in town an overreaction to conditions they were used to.[10]

Toxic runoff from the Bunker Hill mine and other mine operations in the valley also fouled the South Fork of the Coeur d'Alene River, Lead Creek in my lexicon, and other creeks in the valley running into the river. The damage this pollution did was recognized as early as 1902, when mine owners in the valley bought out farmers and leased back the land to avoid litigation from floods depositing tailings, destroying the land value for agriculture. Bunker Hill did take steps as early as 1927 to try and reduce the amount of pollution from mining operations and processing by building tailings ponds. By 1981, the dike walls had grown to forty feet, surrounding 160 acres of land. Beginning in 1960, Bunker also pumped a good portion of the tailings back into the mines to fill up the mined-out stopes. A water treatment center was built in the 1960s to remove metals in solution from the water being pumped out of the mine.

Through all these years, men continued to drill, blast, and muck out. Millions of dollars worth of metals were taken from the mountains of Kellogg and Bunker Hill's profits continued to grow, as did the town's fortunes. The crises came and went, but the lead and zinc seemed to go on forever. In 1979, one of the newspapers in nearby Spokane printed a four-part series about the mining towns of the Panhandle, emphasizing their wildness, the lack of fear on the part of the miners, the way of life in Kellogg and Wallace.[11] The future looked bright. In an article in another Spokane paper published in January 1980, "Glitter Below Surface in Idaho's Silver Valley," the writer reported that silver production in the valley could reach $1.67 billion in the coming year. Most of the excitement related to the high silver prices during that period, artificially pushed up by speculators in Texas. Nevertheless, the predictions of more "boom time" were high for real estate, miners' wages, and jobs.

Slightly over a year later, Gulf Resources reported it lost $7.7

million in the first half of 1981. Metal prices were too low. The costs of operating, compounded by environmental problems, were too high. The influx of Japanese-imported automobiles was destroying the U.S. market for lead and zinc.

*   *   *

In the summer of 1981, my class held its twentieth high school reunion. For pictures, we grouped together on the lawn at the high school with classes that had been together since grade school. The women still looked good, although the men had begun to gain stomachs and lose hair, but we were all more relaxed, willing to confess a few failures along the way, and talking more about families than careers. By then, I had married again. I didn't bring my husband, Gerry, with me, not wanting to bore him while old friends talked about old times. The boom in Kellogg had disappeared almost overnight, and those who still lived there told us Gulf Resources might close the mine. Few of us took this rumor seriously, yet a cloud hung over our good-byes.

On August 25, 1981, just days after our reunion, Gulf said it would close unless it could get the seven labor unions representing the workers to accept a wage cut of 20 percent. Shock waves reverberated throughout the area. Close? This mine had been in operation almost one hundred years. Surely not! Over two thousand mineworkers would lose their jobs, and the $55 million payroll would disappear. It was unthinkable.

The unions took a vote. Six passed the new contract with the wage cuts. The seventh—the electrical workers—did not. Gulf did what it said it would. Bunker Hill shut down.

Fingers pointed everywhere—at the electrical union for its vote, at the EPA for its unrealistic demands, at Gulf itself for mining the richest, easiest veins first and leaving the less profitable mining for later years, thereby increasing the already high costs of mining.

The Idaho congressional delegation tried to get new tariffs placed on metals from other countries. They urged the EPA to loosen its requirements and extend compliance deadlines. Nothing worked.

Last-ditch efforts to find a buyer for Gulf, to relax environmental requirements, and to get the workers to reduce their wages began again, not by Gulf but by Kellogg residents. But no one wanted this environmental disaster and its attendant liabilities; Gulf had tried for two years to find a buyer. The miners hadn't believed Gulf Resources would close the mine. A short shutdown was all that would happen, they were convinced.

And then a "white knight" appeared on the scene. Several prominent local and Idaho businessmen said they would try to buy Bunker Hill from Gulf if several conditions were satisfied, including limitations on environmental liability, acceptable financing, and new labor agreements with all seven unions, which had to include a wage cut of 25 percent, effective immediately. A publicity and advertising blitz directed to the mine workers and the crafts unions, including the United Steel Workers of America, advanced. At the eleventh hour, all of the local unions voted to take cuts. And then the national United Steel Workers union hierarchy said it would not accept any pay cuts, no matter how the men had voted. It would set a bad precedent for other locations. Perhaps, too, they remembered how a national union had been ousted in favor of a local union in 1960.

In Seattle, I received a telephone call from one of the townspeople desperately seeking legal help to force the national union to accept the local members' decisions. The group already had able legal help. There was nothing I could do except give the name of still another labor lawyer. The man who called me, the grandson of Joe Rinaldi, the Italian stonemason who began working in Kellogg in 1909, cried as he told me what was happening. When I hung up, I, too, cried. This seemed the end of Kellogg.

I didn't want to live in Kellogg, but in many senses it was still home. I'd grown up there, played Indian on the hill, raced my

Schwinn bike down McKinley, looked for frogs in the cattail-lined creek below the mill, marched in the band on the football field, and played in the pep band in the gymnasium. Our stunning metal and glass high school—what would happen to it now? I thought about the backdrop I'd painted for *Finian's Rainbow*, a senior class musical, and all the hours I'd spent in the school—studying, gossiping, flirting. Even the ratty old stuffed wildcat held a fond memory for me—it was the symbol of our school and of the school annual on which I'd worked for three years. What would happen to all the teachers? The ones I'd loved like Miss Rainbolt, Mrs. Gibson, and Mrs. Kenyon, three of my English and literature teachers; Mrs. Fee, with all her quirks; Mr. Thompson, who taught me to type and thereby helped me support myself when I was a single mother; Mr. Exum, who on his own initiative had written a glowing letter of recommendation to help me get into law school. And all my friends who still lived there.

Even after the mines closed, efforts continued to reopen the workings. The pumps continued to pump water, but then the sinter plant was sold to a mining company in Mexico. The EPA came in and threw fences around the whole area and declared it to be a Superfund site, requiring anywhere from $55 million to $120 million to clean up. The smelter was dismantled and then the zinc plant.

When I descended the mine in 1990, very limited work continued via an independent contractor. No smelting facilities were available, but the ore could be shipped out of state for processing. This work, too, stopped.

The final blow came when the electricity for the pumps was turned off in the mid-1990s. Washington Water Power bills had not been paid for some time. Once the pumps ceased, the workings flooded. The mines were closed forever.

Or so I thought. With the lower levels flooded, some work has continued sporadically in the levels above the Kellogg entrance by contract miners and small operators. The number of men still employed from time to time ranges from 50 to 150. Because the rockhouse burned and there was no longer a mill, it didn't make sense that anyone would try to mine, but from time to time, when I drove down McKinley to where the fence stopped me, I could see that there were cars parked around the mine entrance.

For years, the men stayed in Kellogg, waiting for the mines to reopen. Unemployment rates grew to over 50 percent, and still they stayed. Some traveled to mines in Montana or Wyoming or Nevada, but those mines, too, closed down or continued only limited operations. The men came back home to Kellogg and waited. The Sunshine Mine closed when the silver prices dove, but it still operated from time to time when silver reached five dollars an ounce. Then there were jobs for the miners who waited.

Every April, the Old-Timers' Club meets. Virl took me to one of the meetings. Anyone who worked in the area mines was eligible to join. In the lower level of the Elks Club, the same place our high school reunions convened, a dozen tables were set up for dinner. After a cocktail hour in which half a dozen former miners offered to buy me drinks, we all sat down. Another half-dozen had come up to me to say that "Doc Whitesel was my doctor. He was a great guy." I sat between Virl and Dee, who had driven the forty-odd miles from his small farm north of Coeur d'Alene. I recognized several "old-timers" as classmates when I was in high school.

The guest speaker that night was a former engineer. He described how the Kellogg Tunnel was built at the turn of the twentieth century and noted several other milestones for the men: rock bolting began during World War II, and in 1975 the first woman worked underground as a miner. Then he launched into the nicknames for the men: Shotgun, Bastard John, Boots, Slippers, Dirty Dick, Skidrow, Pickles, Mustard, Pork Chops, Ajax, Farmer.

After dinner, one of the men held up his forearm for me to see. "See that?" he asked.

I didn't see anything to remark upon, but said, "A strong arm. Did you work underground?"

He shook his arm. "Yup, but that isn't what I wanted you to notice. I was doing timber repair and a ten-inch-thick piece of shape ripped my arm open so the skin and muscle was hanging off it. I looked at it, lit a cigarette, and walked a mile to the hoist. Then I showered before the company ambulance took me to your dad. He stitched it up—eighty-five stitches." He rolled his arm. "No scar." All I could think about was the long walk with blood dripping.

"You should of seen his hand shake. But when he started stitching, he was a rock."

24

This Lake Is Contaminated

"Love Canal probably never saw anything like this."

George Gunderson

For dozens of years, the black slag pile occupied a mile-long stretch of land beside I-90 just outside Smelterville. Every year for almost a century, eleven thousand pounds of lead were dumped into Lead Creek from active mines in the Silver Valley. Even after the Bunker Hill closed, the heavy metals runoff continued at a high rate. This toxic runoff destroyed aquatic life for years and seeped its way to Coeur d'Alene Lake, thirty miles to the west, where reportedly a witch's brew of lead, mercury, and cadmium rest on the bottom of the lake. Farm animals and domestic fowl—geese, cows, horses—and wild birds have all died from ingesting the water.

After the smelter closed in 1981, as reported in the *Idaho Statesman* in January 1990, the Environmental Protection Agency found buried caches:

- Three hundred tons of mercury sludge
- Fifty tons of magnesium and another thirty tons of mercury
- Two one-ton lead buttons dumped in settling ponds
- Industrial waste piles containing arsenic in concentrations of two hundred thousand parts per million

The EPA declared the twenty-one-square-mile Bunker Hill mining area centered in Kellogg as a Superfund site, the second-largest such site in the country. Clean-up efforts began in the 1980s and continued to the turn of the century. Over $200 million will have been spent, with two million cubic yards of contaminated soil removed, including the dirt from the yards of two thousand residents, which was replaced with clean dirt and seeded with grass. On many of my visits to Kellogg in the 1990s, heavy machinery was at work in one neighborhood after another. Most of the people I talked with considered this effort to be expensive at best and ridiculous at worst.

Most of the contaminated materials came from the Smelterville Flats along Lead Creek. Almost thirty thousand cubic yards of mine tailings were removed each week of the project, and this did not include materials in the 160 acres of tailings ponds. Talk I heard suggested that a golf course was going to be planted over the ponds.

In the summers of 1997 and 1998, "Port-a-dam" tarps were used to rechannel the river in order to remove material from the riverbed. Then Superfund clean-up crews worked to reshape the river to its original, meandering flow. The old lead smelter was demolished and removed and the site capped with layers of slag material which acts much like sand, then a polyethylene liner stretched across it, followed by six inches of topsoil and grass. By the summer of 2001, thick grass grew on the smelter site, and the slag pile sported a cap of baby green blades.

When the baghouse burned in 1974, the EPA closed the Silver King grade school, up a gulch between Smelterville and Kellogg, due to elevated lead levels in the blood of the students. The *Idaho Statesman*, a Boise newspaper, reported that 98 percent of the 175 children examined within one mile of the smelter complex had blood-lead levels of eighty micrograms or more, that is, lead poisoning. Lead exposure "has to be considered a two-generational disease for women," according to Dr. John Rosen, a pediatric specialist on lead-related research for Albert Einstein College of Medicine in New York City.[12] The health problems included cancer, kidney stones, nervous system disorders, hypertension, and painful joints. Dyslexia or learning disorders and low IQ were also problems.

Town residents voted by 88 percent to reopen the school within months of its closure. When the mine shut down, the school closed again due to dwindling student population. People didn't believe the lead levels. After all, most of them had lived near the smelter all their lives, and few of them had suffered the effects the EPA warned about. Thousands of students had attended college, earned degrees, returned to Kellogg or worked elsewhere, leading productive lives.

I left Kellogg before the huge emissions of lead in 1974. Nevertheless, I breathed in the sulfur dioxide, lead particles, and whatever else was released in the "normal" course of the mining operations. While I don't think I suffered ill effects, nor did most of my contemporaries, there are unexplained cancer clusters—four incidents of cancer in one family a block from my house where the father regularly entered the mine as an engineer, and several other cases of cancer in my small neighborhood. My own daughter suffered dyslexia while growing up, a problem we struggled with for years. These cases don't add up to a verifiable statistic, but there are other examples. Consider the high rate of multiple sclerosis in the Idaho Panhandle and around Spokane, one of the highest in the nation. Two of my senior class died from the disease, one within years of graduation, one years later. Also, respiratory and lung cancer rates were double the state average between 1977 and 1986 in Shoshone County where Kellogg is located.[13]

During the clean-up, fences surrounded the entire Bunker Hill operation from just past the mine entrance on McKinley Avenue to the road leading up to Silver Creek where the zinc plant used to stand, across the valley to the far side of the slag heap next to the freeway. Signs warned people to keep out or they would suffer instant poisoning.

Signs were also posted by the lower end of Coeur d'Alene Lake and by other small lakes in the area:

WARNING: This lake is contaminated with lead and other metals from mine tailings. Small children are at greatest risk. To protect your health, avoid breathing dust and touching the soil and mud. Wash hands before eating and serving foods. Do not eat large amounts of fish, waterfowl or aquatic plants. Do not drink water from the river or lakes.

When the mines closed, area residents began to look for alternative businesses to support the town. A major effort resulted in an upgrading of the ski area on Wardner Peak, first known as Jackass Ski Bowl after Noah Kellogg's burro, later as Silverhorn and finally, now, as Silver Mountain. In keeping with the Bavarian theme adopted when the "longest gondola in the Western hemisphere" (paid for in part by $2 million awarded by Congress) was about to be installed, the town built a Tyrolean base structure to house the lower end of the gondola. Soon, storefronts and new buildings sported the alpine theme—flowers painted across their fronts, carved wood gables, flower pots hanging from streetlights.

Bare mountain slopes belied any effort to mimic alpine ski villages. The slag heap at the entrance to town would not go away quickly, if ever, although major inroads were made in its size. The gondola structure on the town's lower level has been the destination for skiers, not the main business area on the upper level. The banner announcing uptown Kellogg as a Bavarian village hung lifelessly across the street on McKinley Avenue, just in front of the abandoned YMCA with its square brick profile and boarded-up windows. Few of the businesses uptown ever seemed busy with customers, in spite of the flowers and scallops on their fake gables. Cafes have come and gone and the only one with longevity was the hamburger joint.

Wallace has been more successful in its campaign to attract tourists. It bills itself as an old mining town, when in fact little mining ever took place there. Nevertheless, tourists can take a ride into a mine, visit the Oasis Bordello Museum, and visit another museum with old mining equipment and a diorama or two. A Molly B'Damm Motel, commemorating Burke's early madam, attracts customers. Several movies have been filmed in the town, including *Heaven's Gate* and *Dante's Peak*.

Many of us who left Kellogg wondered why the town fathers didn't gravitate to a mining theme for Kellogg's rebirth. The trip into the main hoistroom at the Kellogg entrance to Bunker Hill provides a real look at a famous mine. The possibilities for reenactment of the labor wars up to 1899 could have been capitalized upon.

As part of the Bavarian theme, Silver Mountain expanded its operations from Wardner Peak to Kellogg Peak, both snow-covered all winter long. This was made possible by government funds and a bond passed by the strapped townspeople. The town built a new lodge, created a grassy amphitheatre and added new chairlifts. A successful entrepreneur from Coeur d'Alene offered his company as the marketing agent, and for several years, the ski area at least seemed to hover on the brink of becoming a recognized small resort. But it was small and few lodgings were available. If the winters were successful, the summers were not. Although residents of surrounding towns attended concerts in the amphitheater and tourists stopped to take summer rides on the gondola to the mountain tops, not enough spent the kind of money necessary to keep Kellogg going. Certainly, a tourist industry could not replace the high wages and the huge payroll the mines had provided. The ski area for a time had difficulty supporting itself. The company that manufactured the gondola and owned a major interest in the operations, decided to sell out. Another company bought the gondola, promising to keep it in place for five years.

In summer 2001, the owner of Silver Mountain announced new expansion plans for the ski area and additional recreation facilities to make the area a "four seasons" resort.

Maybe the predictions were wrong. Kellogg would not become a ghost town.

25

I Do Know Where
I Came From

Returning band members mingled on the vacant lot where grass grew in bunches, green as it should be in August. Concrete chunks and weathered asphalt reminded us where the old brick high school once stood, with its three stories of yawning windows, canted and varnished wood floors, and corridors crowded with teenagers smelling like wet wool and hair goo. Instruments, their lyres stuffed with music, hung loosely in our hands. While we waited to march, we mixed in a slow quadrille, discovering friends we hadn't seen in years, recalling musical successes at the festival in Lewiston and the seven-mile Lilac Days' parades in Spokane, where we scalded and blistered our feet. No one could forget the half-time drills in mud or snow on the football field and the shoes we threw away, nor the pep band fight songs to spur our basketball team to yet another state championship.

We recounted accomplishments in the intervening years and compared distances we traveled to this Kellogg All-School Reunion in 1986. Graduates from over a fifty-year time span, including those of my class of 1961, had come to celebrate our town and to remember its heydays when the mines still disgorged ore out of the mountains to be smelted and refined, then sent into the world as lead pigs, zinc bars, and silver ingots. I was afraid this might be the last time I saw Kellogg. Already the foundations were rusting and weakening, barely noticeable that day. Would they soon be covered over with time and dust until the town that raised me would be swallowed by the earth and sky?

Clear air and sunshine belied the sadness shading the edges of our conversations. Nostalgia for the smelter smoke even made the rounds. Evergreen trees, planted in 1981 by the football team and Boy Scouts on the bare and still toxic hillsides, were hardly five feet tall. Some of the band members and former students who lived in Kellogg still waited for the mines to reopen so men and sometimes women could go back underground and make a decent living, so the blank storefronts with cracked windows would be repaired, so the welfare checks in town could be replaced with hard-earned dollars. The town wasn't dead yet, but the prognosis wasn't good, as my father would have said.

*   *   *

On the night before the reunion parade, we band members met in the gym of the new junior high school situated near Lead Creek, no longer filled with tailings. It looked almost clear. The band leader was someone we didn't know, but he'd studied under Mr. Exum, so we knew he was a good musician. We would practice, he said, before marching the next day on our old route from the top of Main Street, turning on McKinley and then down to the football field for a short concert. Did we all have our music? "Stars and Stripes Forever," a John Philip Sousa march, and "Tequila," a football audience favorite, and "On Wisconsin," better known to us as "Go You Wildcats." He was certain, he said, that we would all remember our fight song and alma mater, "Hail to the Wildcats." I hummed the next line to myself, "long may you reign supreme," to prove it so.

We had sorted ourselves into sections in the music room—woodwinds in the first two rows on either side, saxophones behind the flutes, small brass in the middle, then in third and fourth tiers, the big brass, with drums, snare and bass, around the outer perimeter of the half circle. Alan, my old nemesis in flute competition, was there, no longer round and pasty-faced, but tall, lean, and sweet, offering me the first chair I'd abandoned to join the drill team. I declined. He deserved it. Other flute players, only some of whom we both knew, graciously took seats three through six or seven. I wondered if they had even heard of the hard-fought battles between Alan and me. No doubt, we were just strangers, as they were to us.

I looked around and saw the adult forms of the boys I once admired and secretly hoped to impress when I was a junior high school girl and they were high school "men." They were real men now, thicker and taller with gray in their thinning hair. The girls were women with stories I knew. Sylvia was back from Africa where she had stayed after years in the Peace Corps; Kathy practiced law on the East Coast; Gayle developed computer programs for teaching; and Diane still lived in Kellogg, taking care of her parents and helping her husband weather the close-down of the mine. We all had stories that had nothing to do with Kellogg and everything to do with Kellogg.

My flute felt warm in my hands. Mother had retrieved it from the basement where it was stored along with relief maps of Peru and Florida, carefully written reports in artful folders about Australia and Aztecs and The Everglades, and faded report cards. She also sent my marching songs, five-by-eight-inch pages of notation, and a music book with flute fingering on the back page. Practicing in my basement in Seattle, finding the old fingering and remembering the notes, brought back to me the mornings in Senior Band. The room had been bright and cheerful while outside snow fell, rains poured, smelter lights cut the darkness, and yellow school buses crept up the gulch to drop off students for classes.

And then Mr. Exum came into the room—standing tall, his crisp mustache unchanged, his twinkly eyes still gleaming. Affection for him flooded through me, as if I had never hated the discipline, the sometimes arbitrary and scornful mien he presented to us. He had demanded so much and expected even more.

"Hope for the best," he used to say almost every morning, "but be prepared for the worst."

Everyone stood and clapped and whistled. He smiled, pleased at the tribute, and I saw that he, too, had changed. In his summer shirt, his arms, once muscled and wiry had thinned to slack ropes, the fringe of hair around his head was even more sparse and gray, his cheeks gaunt and lined as if from constant grimace. Stomach troubles, we'd heard. Maybe cancer. He was coming. He wasn't coming. And there he was. He lifted a broken drum stick and rapped the music stand. We all laughed at this signal to "sit straight, pay attention, breathe deeply, play."

He looked around the room, saying hello to the people who had once been his students, the ones he'd taught year after year during fall, winter, and spring and left behind every year after summer band to climb peaks in the Grand Tetons. And then he turned to me.

"Julie, your obligato in the William Tell Overture in Lewiston was the most beautiful I ever heard." He bowed to me. I struggled not to spring into tears and I bowed my head to him. Thirty years ago, I'd faced his anger and disbelief when I quit band. Over the years since, I'd learned how important were the lessons he taught us. What he said had mattered, and still did. A thrill moved my heart.

Mr. Exum lifted his arms. We raised our instruments in one motion and we played.

*   *   *

Next day, we lined up on the street and marched. We strutted as if this were something each of us had done once a week since we graduated, although the old toe-heel motion didn't work as well in loafers and sport shoes. Alan's piccolo notes soared like a singing bird. We passed the *Kellogg Evening News* office; the city hall and police station; the McConnell Hotel dark and deserted like the old flophouse that it was; Joe & Henry's pool room, Morrow's Clothing Store, Damiano's drugstore. The remembered smell of toasted cheese sandwiches and Green River phosphates hovered in my imagination. Sunlight reflecting off metal sparkled in the store windows. Between songs, our feet shuffled in cadence on pavement. Another Sousa march and we lifted our knees higher, played louder, wanting to fill the valley with triumphant noise.

Around the corner we marched, our lines bending and straggling. I caught a glimpse of Bob Robson's office, where I'd worked so hard and learned so much. I believed then that I helped rescue the town from a nine-month strike that nearly destroyed it. The closing of the Bunker Hill mine in 1981 should have been the final straw, but still the town struggled for life. Under us, thousands of feet below, pumps labored to keep the drifts open, just in case. Just in case the prices of lead and zinc improved, the regulators changed their minds about pollution, the unions agreed to lower wages. Just in case the New York and California shareholders voted in a miracle.

People crowded the sidewalks—the majority of returning graduates who didn't play in the band and residents of the town. They waved, and we waved. In spite of my practice, I didn't know many of the notes and I didn't own a lyre. Only Alan knew all the music by memory. I watched my row, making certain I was in line and not out of step, forgetting that now most of us were out of step with Kellogg.

At the end of McKinley lay the entrance to the mine, a place few of us had visited, not even the boys who worked summers at the zinc plant. Evidence of the mines was at hand, however, in the sparse vegetation, the number of bars, the weary faces of some members of the audience, even in the absence of miners and those injured or killed on the job. Our music thinned. Donna's Dresses and Mode O'Day were gone, but the doors of Kellogg Billiards and the Rio Bar stood wide open, country music spilling out. The street we marched on was old and ribboned with cracks. Empty storefronts were beginning to encroach on the center intersection like a form of black death creeping.

Tootle tootle. Boom boom. Ra ta ta ta ta. Just like the old days. We wore our reunion T-shirts, emblazoned with a drawing of the steel and glass high school that had replaced the brick one. At Hill Street, we turned the corner again at the far end of the football stadium, marched down and onto the field. The stands began to fill with former students and current townspeople. We grinned at their clapping, a close relative to the hand-pounding for the football players of old. Then Mr. Exum came onto the field in the back of a convertible, and the slap of flesh grew into low thunder. He climbed out, stepped up to the podium, and once again raised his hands. For the very last time, we lifted our instruments and played.

Many of my old girlfriends came to the reunion or still lived in Kellogg. After the parade and before the barbecue and dance on the football field, we met at a cafe in the converted union hall by the railroad tracks. We sat in plastic chairs at plastic tables and dawdled over Cokes and coffee.

One friend waved her hand across the table. "Look! I'm engaged!" Her diamond was the size of a large gold nugget.

"Who is he?" "Where did you meet him?" "Is he from California?" We all talked at once. We knew she was divorced from the husband she married in college, that she had lived in Hawaii for a while and now taught school in California.

"I met him on an airplane," she said and giggled. "He's a huge computer expert, and—" —(sotto voce) "I'm living with him." She told a few more details and the conversation shifted.

"You know, my memories of Kellogg are all so good," Kathy said. "We had a special life growing up here, didn't we? I wonder if it all was as wonderful as it seemed."

I remembered Kathy, her sister, and her parents walking or driving in their old Studebaker past our house every night to go to one of the cafes uptown or in Sunnyside for dinner. Her mother didn't cook. I mentioned this and added, "Do you cook, Kathy?" We laughed.

"Yes, but I must say that with Robert and I both commuting to New York City to work and with the children so busy with school and activities, I get help to clean and do the cooking." She paused a moment as if to weigh her next words. "My mother didn't cook much because the kitchen sink was always full of dirty dishes and the counters had moldy food on them. We almost had to go somewhere else to eat."

Sylvia stepped into the silence. "My mother taught me how to cook. And every summer, she went to Moscow to school and I took care of my father. I missed her so much, but I did love taking care of him and spending so much time up the river."

"I'm envious of your mother and father, Sylvia," I said. "And yours, too, Kathy. My mother's kitchen was clean, but I was scared to death of my father. He drank at night and ranted at us. He called us terrible names and accused me of—" I stopped, then continued. "Some of the very worst times were around the dinner table. I can remember wishing I was walking with your family to dinner, Kathy."

Diane said, "I sometimes wished my mother would say anything. She would get mad at my dad or one of us and not speak for days and weeks at a time."

We remembered friends who hadn't come—Betty, who lived in the Caribbean; Gary, who was recovering from cancer treatment; and others. A friend who died of MS, a favorite teacher who finally found love with another woman and then died of a cerebral hemorrhage, and the dentist who killed himself. Later that night, several of us continued talking at the little trailer owned by Sylvia's family along the North Fork of the Coeur d'Alene River. Sharing our secrets brought relief and sisterhood under the stars flickering through the cottonwood branches, next to water that smelled green and pure.

Next day, we cheered at the "junior-senior" basketball game in the high school gym; drank beer in the back room at Joe & Henry's, the bar where we "nice" girls had never gone; sat on a stool at Kellogg Billiards next to Bones Davis, our small-town male Dear Abby. I talked with friends, young and old, at the barbecue, and drank outside of Dirty Ernie's, a tavern owned by a classmate, and danced in the street. Almost forgotten thoughts and feelings slipped in and out of my memory: a breaking heart, fear of and shame over my father's drinking, humiliation at being skinny and unasked at long-ago dances, pride at doing a job well in a lawyer's office, jealousy of pretty girls, trepidation as I prepared my valedictory speech for graduation. These were my Idaho tailings.

To paraphrase Wallace Stegner, if I haven't always known who I was or am, I do know where I came from: Kellogg, a small mining town in northern Idaho.

26

Uncle Bunker Is Dead

Shortly after the appointed hour on that Memorial Day in 1996, we saw billows of smoke appear around the base of the shortest smokestack, followed by more clouds around the next highest stack—the two older chimneys near the zinc plant and behind the smelter. A popping sound like summer firecrackers drifted toward us, and then the stacks crumbled in on themselves in a silent avalanche of brick and dust, as if they had been built without mortar. The shorter was around 250 feet; the taller, 500 feet.

After a brief wait, more smoke and this time a rumbling sound came from the third stack, the 610-foot acid plant chimney. It toppled over sideways, just like a Ponderosa pine dropping to the earth. Again, no noise accompanied the plunging giant, reminding me of the old riddle: If a tree falls in the forest, does it make a sound if no one is there? Thousands of people were watching this chimney, and no one said a word. When it hit the ground, a *crump* followed several seconds later.

Smoke plumed up from the base of the tallest and nearest stack, and then we heard the *boom boom* of the dynamite. The stack stood, not wavering so much as an inch. We looked at each other, thinking something had gone wrong. The watchers collectively held their breath.

Finally, the 715-foot concrete column canted to the side. It hesitated and leaned more. It began to slip sideways, a giant concrete tree falling. The sound of the explosion had passed beyond us; the silence felt strange, as if we were watching an old-time movie. When the stack reached a 45-degree angle, the concrete broke in the middle, and both pieces continued their sidelong plunge. They bounced in a storm of dust, shaking the earth in a way the explosions had not.

Almost everyone cheered. I did not.

Trenches dug for the two largest chimneys had been lined with layers of plastic. Both smokestacks, their insides coated with arsenic, lead, and chemicals that had steamed through them, rested in the trenches, like bodies in coffins. The long slits would be covered over, and the poisons would be forever contained.

People in cars zipping along on I-90 on their way to somewhere else would never know why the town was there, how wild and wide-open it once was, how many riches had been taken from the mountains and turned into products, perhaps even supplying zinc and lead for the automobiles in which they drove. They would see a medium-wide river and ordinary-looking mountains, Monopoly-sized houses going up the hill on one side of the interstate and filling the valley on the other side. Perhaps someone would notice the green trees and grass of the cemetery above the town. The Miner's Hat Realty, round and brimmed like a true miner's hat sitting at the eastern edge of town, might spark a comment. Zip, zip past town and on to Wallace with its greener hillsides and then on to the Montana border.

I felt a lump in my throat. I looked around at the others. Everyone waited for something else to happen. Nothing did. Slowly, we picked up our belongings and began the hike back to our cars. I saw a few solemn faces, older faces, and the shine of a tear. My face was wet, too, in a farewell to the mines and the community where my family had lived, where my father had doctored for over thirty years, where I had come of age. Kellogg's monuments were gone.

Uncle Bunker was indeed dead.

Epilogue
Sixty-five Sold in One Day!

Lily pads floated between age-blackened stumps on the slough where I used to ice-skate. Summer heat replaced the winter cold of crack-the-whip and romantic trysts behind frozen cattails. As I entered the west end of the valley, where once I saw bare mountains and smokestacks, I now saw green trees thrusting up along the slopes. For the first time, Silver Valley resembled the landscape around most small towns in northern Idaho.

At Smelterville, I left the interstate to see for myself what I had been told by friends. "The town is booming." "Condominiums are sprouting everywhere." "A Wal-Mart is moving in." Good news to those who mentioned it. My last visit of several years ago sprang to mind: deserted streets, grass growing in cracks in the sidewalks, dust blowing off the flats near where I now drove.

The old road was familiar enough. It wound past the slough, edged the tailings ponds—still elevated behind dirt and clay walls— and past the road to Page, where trees lined the way up the hill. The Boat Drive-in, where my friends and I always went for sodas, shakes, and burgers after basketball and football games and after dances looked spiffed up but less like a boat than ever.

Then I entered Smelterville. Or maybe it was vice versa. Even the outer edges of the town lay crumbled in ruins and desolation. Tattered remnants sank into the red sand like so many sticks. Taverns and stores I remembered from days of traveling through to skate or flirt with boys at the Boat stood shuttered with broken windows, caved-in doors and roofs. Beyond Main Street, people did still live in this town, but I didn't turn off to see, afraid of what I might find. At the edge of town stood the slag heap, its burnt black sands disguised by grass. It looked like a natural piece of landscape, a place where someone might build a house to gain a view. Of trees.

In the past couple of decades, the road winding from Smelterville to Kellogg was closed by a chain link fence, prohibiting passage through the Superfund site remaining when the mines closed. Today, nothing barred the way—a pleasant surprise. Up Government Gulch, the zinc plant had been dismantled and the hillside lay empty. Smelter Heights, where mine managers and supervisors once lived, reminded me of an overgrown battlefield. The gracious Cape Cod and colonial-style houses had been scraped years ago and the remaining mounds and pits sprouted weeds, yellowed bunch grass, and a few bushes.

More grass covered everything else. Gone were the ramshackle houses where lead-poisoned children had lived. Their families were awarded large amounts in a lawsuit against Bunker Hill but many left before they collected their judgments. Gone were the smelter and baghouse, the mill and rockhouse. Not a piece of concrete or metal flange marred the fields lining both sides of the road, running up to the foot of the sidehills on the right and down to the empty holding pond area on the left. The smokestacks disappeared years ago.

I felt tears gathering. The blues that seeped into me as I drove through Smelterville failed to dissipate as I passed the clean grassy heights. Instead, the sorrow grew. Surely, I could not be nostalgic for arsenic and sulfurous smoke; for leaded- and cyanide-leached ground; for bare, etched hillsides.

Across the valley in the distance, rows and rows of brand new

trucks and SUVs lined up like soldiers, gleaming in the sunny afternoon. Dave Smith Motors—"The Home of Hassle Free Buying"—is
Kellogg's largest business and employer. This company sells vehicles to people all over the West. Overhead, the gondola cars creaked
on cables to rise to the ski lodge at the base of Kellogg Peak. The
aging yellow brick Bunker Hill office building, two stories high
with black windows facing McKinley Avenue, appeared forlorn
and empty. The town council was considering a variance to local
zoning rules for a developer to build a four- or five-story condominium complex. There hardly appeared room, unless the razing included a ramshackle house where my lawyer boss once lived.

A medical office complex filled the parking lot across from where
the hospital once stood. Farther along, Lincoln School, too, stood
silent with boards on all the windows. Faded signs told of one
reincarnation as a "mall," also now gone. The next plan is for "Lincoln Lofts," with more condominiums inside its red brick exterior.
Down the hill, past the football field—newly furbished and waiting
for fall games—construction activity filled the air with hammering
and buzzing and dust and economic excitement. Morning Star
Lodge, an extensive condominium development by Eagle Crest, the
purchaser of the ski operation several years earlier, surrounded the
base of the gondola. "Sixty-five sold in one day!" boasted a local.

Up Jacobs Gulch, I visited the still modern high school. The
scowling wildcat behind the neon dressing must have been recently painted. The windows sparkled. Even the grass was cut. I
could feel the old excitement of a new school year. I parked my car
to look across the valley. No smelter, no smoke, and no lights.
Instead, Haystack Peak shone in the sunlight with evergreens from
bottom to top.

I thought of the spring when we students worked on a project to
build a K there. We painted two-by-ten boards and carried them up
the steep hillside past my old Indian village. The wood letter, posi-

tioned high on bare slopes of former days, would not be visible now even if it existed. Instead, a new *K* perched at the top of the rounded peak, a silhouette against the southern sky.

I drove past Dave Smith Motors, spread across four or five blocks of Sunnyside. Its lots were like the ant farms we used to get for Christmas, with buyers and salespeople climbing in and out of vans and trucks and other gas guzzlers. The price of gas appeared to make no difference to this commercial endeavor. Up Division and up Wardner I toured to check out former stomping grounds. Wardner was the first town in this end of Silver Valley and still a separate township from Kellogg, merging where the old high school had been dismantled, brick by brick, and never replaced. I expected another Smelterville and instead found newer cedar and log houses, a number of vacant lots smoothed over and growing grass, and a sign for a new Wardner Canyon homes development. A few of the older houses from mining days—small cottages whose doors opened directly into a living room with two or three bedrooms in back—had been re-sided or painted and shone along with the new.

The weight centering around my heart lifted a little, only to fall again when I drove through the center of downtown Kellogg. Although the drugstore still retained its hold on the corner of Main and McKinley, and the library had expanded to fill what was the city hall—now moved into the mine offices at the other end of town—the drive down McKinley was again a trip past empty storefronts and unbusy businesses. The Alpine Village, named in the banner across the street, offered little to anyone who ventured there. Maybe the story changed when winter and skiing tourists arrived.

I left town and stopped to see my friend Diane at her summer cabin. We sat in a lawn swing where we could stay in the shade and smell fresh, mowed grass and watch sunlight on the lake below. She had recently suffered a stroke and carefully chose her words. Her always lovely dark eyes and glowing skin were unchanged. Her husband, Bernard, tall and aging from his own health problems, cared for her and her ancient father, Chuck Biotti. At ninety-four, he crouched forward when he walked, but he was still lively and interested in the world around him.

"What do you think about town?" Diane asked.

"Lots of building going on."

"A new development of houses, really big houses, went in at Page," Diane said. We talked about who still lived in town and who didn't. Which houses had become bed and breakfast lodgings. Which restaurants closed and what filled their places.

Diane and Bernard described the Eagle Crest development. A second phase—maybe it was a third phase—of one hundred condominiums was planned. An indoor water park would lure tourists to the new Morning Lodge Hotel at the base of the gondola. I had heard a golf course was going in on the tailings ponds, but no, the golf course would be sited where the smelter and other mining buildings had reigned along McKinley, where grass now grew. "It is going to be a four seasons resort."

Chuck missed the mining activity. The highline train he ran had disappeared years ago. "I'm busy with my garden now." His garden covered half an acre of ground between the cabins and a field where cows grazed. "I heard Sunshine Mine might be operated again," he said.

"A leach plant is supposed to go in up near Murray," Diane's husband said. "There's a copper-silver deposit around there." He shook his head. So did I. More poisons in the soil. Just what a Superfund site needed.

Diane's twin grandchildren, aged three, swarmed around, climbing on and over Chuck. Their mother, Mary, joined us. "What do you think about town?"

Again, I avoided giving a direct answer. I needed to think about what I had just seen. My face must have shown my ambivalence.

"It means lots of jobs," she said. "The economy is springing back." Diane's son served on the town council and was deeply involved in planning and zoning. Mary's voice reflected the optimism of youth. Maybe that would revive the area.

As I drove away, I still felt blue. Diane's health worried and saddened me, too. Mary made me realize that what was happening in Kellogg was good news, a good thing, for what had been a dying town. Diane, her husband, her father and I were remnants of the old days. What fueled my blues was that Kellogg was no longer *my* town. It is rising as a different town, and more, I hope, than a Dave Smith parking lot. Far from being gone, the good times are just beginning, again.

Notes

Chapter 2 epigraph: Campbell and Reid state: "The rocks of the Coeur d'Alene Mining District have been intensely deformed in a complex pattern that shows a marked disclosure of structural elements on opposite sides of the Osburn Fault and which well might be referred to as a structural knot."

1. Campbell and Reid, *Idaho Bureau of Mines*.

2. Coeur d'Alene means "heart of an awl" in French. Early French traders applied this name to the Native Americans in the area, referring to what they considered sharp trading practices.

3. See Holbrook, *The Rocky Mountain Revolution*.

4. Nearly all of the statistics concerning the Bunker Hill mine in this chapter and in later chapters are derived from *"Uncle Bunker": Memories in Words and Pictures,* by Ray Chapman, and from the *Bunker Hill Reporter*, a newsletter published by the Bunker Hill Mining Company and edited by Ray Chapman.

5. Most of the mine is now closed completely and the lower tunnels flooded with water. The processing buildings have been dismantled and grass has been planted over the entire outside area, including on the slag pile. It is difficult to see that the Bunker Hill Mine ever existed.

6. Possibly Herb Philbrick, who was an undercover agent for the FBI in the late 1940s. A television series, *I Led Three Lives*, popular during this period, portrayed Philbrick's experiences.

7. Elizabeth Fee wrote her master's thesis at the University of Idaho on the 1960 strike. She credited the students and the I Am An Ameri-

can Youth Group as a key element in getting the strike settled. Her conviction that the Mine Mill Union had Communist connections never wavered.

8. "Bunker Hill: How It Happened; Idaho's Environmental Nightmare," *Idaho Statesman*, January 28, 1990.

9. See Editorial, "The Awful Lesson of Bunker Hill," *Seattle Post-Intelligencer*, August 1, 1990.

10. "Commissioner Answers NBC News Lead Report," *Kellogg Evening News*, November 28, 1979. The paper highlighted a letter from Bill Noyen, county commissioner, who pointed out that he had lived in the area thirty-three years, his three children were all healthy, and the Bunker had made "immense strides" in improving air quality and living conditions. The Editor's Note said the opinions of Mr. Noyen were "no doubt concurred in by thousands of Silver Valley residents." This letter was written before the public knew of the emissions after the baghouse fire.

11. "Mining Life," *Spokesman-Review*, December 2–5, 1979

Chapter 24 epigraph: George Gunderson, former Bunker Hill employee, gave a list of burial sites of toxic materials to federal environmental authorities and was quoted in the *Idaho Statesman*, January 28, 1990.

12. *Idaho Statesman*, January 28, 1990.

13. Ibid.

Bibliography and Further Reading

Printed Sources

Aiken, Katherine. *Idaho's Bunker Hill: The Rise and Fall of a Great Mining Company, 1885–1981.* Norman: University of Oklahoma Press, 2005.

Bankson, Russell A., and Lester S. Harrison. *Beneath These Mountains.* New York: Vantage Press, 1966.

Brainard, Wendell, and Ray Chapman. *Golden History Tales from Idaho's Coeur d'Alene Mining District 1990.* Wallace, Idaho: Crow's Printing.

Campbell, Arthur B., and R. R. Reid. *Idaho Bureau of Mines and Geology, Bulletin no. 16,* 1961.

Chapman, Ray. *History of Idaho's Silver Valley, 1878–2000.* Kellogg, Idaho: Chapman Publishing, 2000.

——. *History of Kellogg, Idaho, 1885–2002.* Kellogg, Idaho: Chapman Publishing, 2002.

——. *"Uncle Bunker": Memories in Words and Pictures.* Kellogg, Idaho: Chapman Publishing, 1994.

Dolph, Jerry. *Fire in the Hole: The Untold Story of Hardrock Miners.* Pullman: Washington State University Press, 1994.

Friedline, Apal A. *Generations.* Caxton Press, privately printed in 1941.

Gold Strikes and Silver Linings: A Collection of Stories on the Development of North Idaho's Mineral Wealth. Silver Valley Economic Development Corporation, 1995.

Hart, Patricia, and Ivar Nelson. *Mining Town: The Photographic Record of*

230 • BIBLIOGRAPHY AND FURTHER READING

T. N. Barnard and Nellie Stockbridge from the Coeur d'Alenes. Seattle and Boise: University of Washington Press and the Idaho State Historical Society, 1984.

Heilbrun, Carolyn G. *Writing a Woman's Life*. New York: Ballantine Books, 1988.

Holbrook, Stewart W. *The Rocky Mountain Revolution*. New York: Henry Holt, 1956.

Kellogg Planning Commission. *The General Plan, Kellogg, Idaho*. April 1, 1957.

Magnuson, Richard G. *Coeur d'Alene Diary: The First Ten Years of Hardrock Mining in North Idaho*. Portland, Ore.: Metropolitan Press, 1968.

Miner's Manual for Spokane and the Coeur d'Alenes, 1969–1970. Published by George Reue, 1969.

Montgomery, James W. *Liberated Woman: a Life of May Arkwright Hutton*. Spokane, Wash.: Gingko House, 1974.

Norlen, Art. *Death of a Proud Union: The 1960 Bunker Hill Strike*. Cataldo, Idaho: Tamarack, 1992.

Olsen, Gregg. *The Deep Dark*. New York: Crown, 2005.

Probert, Alan, ed. *Mining in the West*. Manhattan, Kans.: Sunflower University Press, Journal of the West, Inc., 1981.

Scamahorn, E. D. *The Coeur d'Alene Mining District, as Seen through the Aerial Camera of Scamahorn Air Photo Co*. Spokane, Wash.: Scamahorn Air Photo Co., 1948.

Spencer, Betty Goodwin. *The Big Blowup*. Caldwell, Idaho: Caxton Printers, 1956.

Wolff, Fritz. *A Room for the Summer*. Norman: University of Oklahoma Press, 2005.

Interviews

Conducted between 1989 and 2007
Betty Lou Arens, Seattle, Washington
James Bening, Coeur d'Alene, Idaho (deceased)
Charles Biotti, Kellogg, Idaho (deceased)
Butch Brewer, Spokane, Washington (deceased)
Eunice "Jim" Chilcott, Kellogg, Idaho (deceased)

Hazel Corbeill, Kellogg, Idaho (deceased)
Elizabeth Fee, Wallace, Idaho (deceased)
Eddie Fitzgerald, M.D., Wallace, Idaho (deceased)
Diane Biotti Goodson, Kellogg, Idaho
Janet Hasz, Kellogg, Idaho
Jessie Rinaldi Griffith, Coeur d'Alene, Idaho (deceased)
Virl McCombs, Kingston, Idaho
Harriet McConnell, Kellogg, Idaho (deceased)
Edythe Morbeck, Coeur d'Alene, Idaho (deceased)
Frank Morbeck, Wallace, Idaho (deceased)
William Noyen, Smelterville, Idaho (deceased)
Dolly Parker, Wardner, Idaho (deceased)
Robert M. Robson, Coeur d'Alene, Idaho (deceased)
Rose Rinaldi, Kellogg, Idaho (deceased)
Charles Rinaldi, Kellogg, Idaho (deceased)
Ira D. (Dee) Tatham, Post Falls, Idaho (deceased)
Dora Tatham, Post Falls, Idaho
LaVernon Tuson, Coeur d'Alene, Idaho (deceased)
Marie Haasch Whitesel, Coeur d'Alene, Idaho